Turkish Poetry Today
2016

Turkish Poetry Today

2016

Editors:

Mel Kenne

Saliha Paker

İdil Karacadağ

First published in 2016 by **red hand books**
part of Red Hand Media Ltd
Flexadux House, Grange Road
Gainsborough DN21 1QB

www.redhandbooks.co.uk

Turkish Poetry Today is published annually by
Red hand Books, England

This edition: ISBN 978-1-910346-17-4

A CIP catalogue record for this book is
available from the British Library

Prepared for publication by red hand books
Cover design © red hand books

Contents

A Word from the Editors

To those of you who are already familiar with *Turkish Poetry Today* and to those of you who aren't, to those of you familiar with Turkish poets writing in the present and recent past and to those of you who are not, we bid a hearty welcome to the fourth issue of our journal, which we hope will continue to open doors for all its readers into Turkey's ever-evolving literary scene.

As the new editors of *TPT*, one of the most significant changes we're making is the inclusion of a Featured Poet section that offers a comprehensive selection of a major Turkish poet's work. Our first featured poet, Behçet Necatigil (1916-1979), has long been recognized as a modern Turkish classic, and in this issue you'll encounter the broad range of work produced by this very prolific and versatile writer, comprising not only poems but two essays and an excerpt from his series of highly popular radio plays. We're grateful to the attendees of the 2015 Cunda International Workshop for Translators of Turkish Literature (**tecca.boun.edu.tr**), the focus of which was Behçet Necatigil's writings, for sharing their translations with us.

Following the **Featured Poet** section you'll find a selection of poems that represent the various styles and forms of modern Turkish poetry produced in the last 120 years, including some very recently written work. While, happily enough, the last two or three decades have witnessed an unprecedented surge in the world-wide translation of Turkish poetry and fiction, and some poets of the present generation have been lucky enough to have their work translated and published internationally, Turkish authors haven't always been fortunate enough to be recognized through translations during their lifetime. This means that their work has to wait for 'just the right moment' as the years go by. Fortunately, steady progress is being made in bringing to light the work of highly gifted but woefully overlooked poets (such as that of Behçet Necatigil, Melih Cevdet Anday and others appearing in this journal) to the world outside their native country. We're proud to play a part in this crucial task.

In the third section, devoted to essays and reviews, you'll encounter the review of a collection of poetry by another modern master, Gülten Akın (1933-2015). In a survey sponsored by by the Milliyet Arts Journal in 2008, Gülten Akın was voted 'the greatest living Turkish poet' by an outstanding majority of Turkish writers and critics. Two of her final poems are included in translation in this issue as well. Also, for those who wish to know more about the background of mid-20th century poetics in Turkey we're including an essay famously known in Turkish literary history as '**The Garip Manifesto**' translated by Victoria Holbrook. This extremely important document was written in 1941 by Orhan Veli, who, with young fellow-poets Oktay Rifat and Melih Cevdet Anday, started the *Garip* (Strange) Movement, also known as the First New. A selection of poems by these three poets follows the manifesto, and in the poetry section just before it you'll find several poems by Melih Cevdet Anday translated by Sidney Wade and Efe Murad.

While ideally we might have parallel English/Turkish texts for all contributions, with the expanded content of the journal we only have space for selected bilingual texts interspersed through the first two sections. This will provide an opportunity for readers who are proficient in both English and Turkish to see how the language used by Turkish poets has changed over the decades, and it will show the strategies employed by translators faced with certain problems they encounter vis-à-vis Turkish grammar and colloquial usages.

Our thanks go out to George Messo, Richard Eccles and the other folks at Red Hand Books, first, for making this journal possible, and second, for keeping it going in this fourth year of its publication, a journey already long in the world of literary magazines - particularly of those dedicated to the publication of poetry, and even more so of one dedicated to publishing a poetry that exists on the far boundaries of most English-speaking readers' experience. To us, it's this latter aspect that makes *Turkish Poetry Today* most exciting, for a rich blending of local traditions and modern Western influences is evident in the work of the great diversity of Turkish poets of both sexes writing today. Apropos of poetry written by women we must also thank George Messo for his ground-breaking collection of contemporary poetry by Turkish women *From This Bridge*, which is available from

The Conversation Paperpress. And so we wish you a happy journey as you experience in these pages an 'otherness' of the best type - one not to shrink away from, but rather to learn from and to delight in being drawn into its welcoming embrace.

The Editors

Featured Poet

Behçet Necatigil

Photo by Orhan Murat Arıburnu, 1958

Introducing Behçet Necatigil (1916-1979)

Born in Istanbul in the middle of the First World War and during the final years of the Ottoman Empire, Behçet Necatigil published his first poem in the October 1935 issue of *Varlık* magazine. After his graduation in 1940 from the Istanbul School of Higher Education for Teachers, along with many others of his generation he began his career as a high school teacher in the relatively new Turkish Republic that had been declared in 1923. Thus during his formative years he experienced the social and political turbulence and the resulting radical cultural break that occurred with the country's transformation from empire to nation-state.

His literary education, however, which embraced both the Divan poetry of the Ottomans as well as the poetry of his time, proved to be firmly grounded. In *Edebiyatımızda İsimler Sözlüğü*, the encyclopedic dictionary he published in1960, which is still in print as a classic reference book, he outlined his own poetic career with characteristic modesty as follows:
'In the forty years he spent in poetry, Necatigil drew attention to the circumstances to be encountered by an ordinary individual of moderate means from birth to death, communicating such individuals' real and imagined experiences within the triangle of home, family and immediate environment. At times, some of his innovations in form and style were found to be odd, but critics generally agreed that he was a consistent poet, with a special world of his own' (pp. 278-79).

The last phrase needs a note: when Necatigil was active as young poet in the 1940s, he remained aloof from what was regarded as a radical movement started by the Garip poets because he felt that what they were doing was superficial. Nor was he involved in the socialist poetry of the same period and the 1950s, whose authors were taken to court. On the other hand, he was definitely influenced by the concurrent emergence of the Second New poets who were creating a multitude of innovative forms and metaphoric styles, mainly as a reaction to anti-socialist censorship; yet he stuck to his own path and never became part of their movement.

The corpus of work glossed over by Necatigil as he outlined his career actually comprises more than 13 collections of poetry published between 1945 and 1975. Starting with his first publication in 1935, throughout his life he contributed poems to all the major literary magazines, a number of which didn't appear in his collections. He was awarded the Yeditepe poetry prize for his *Eski Toprak* in 1957 and the Turkish Language Society Poetry prize for *Yaz Dönemi* in 1964.

In the following pages you will find what is meant to be a fairly representative selection from the collected and posthumously published poetry of Behçet Necatigil. You will also find two translations of the poet's well-known essays 'The Houses of the Horoscope of Poetry' and 'I' which sum up his poetics. In the first he traces the mature poet's career through three phases he defines as 'Exile' (*Gurbet*), 'Longing' (*Hasret*) and 'Wisdom' (*Hikmet*). The second, which focuses on the first-person singular 'I' holds the key to many of his enigmatic poems but at the same time poses yet another absorbing puzzle by Necatigil the grammarian. Taken together, these essays illuminate Necatigil's own course of 'forty years in poetry'.

Necatigil's modest summary left out a few other significant aspects of the poet's career that deserve to be mentioned. First of all, Necatigil was a great Turkish literature teacher in some of the best high schools in Istanbul, and memories of him were cherished by his students, some of whom turned out to be poets and critics themselves. Teaching also fuelled his scholarship and literary criticism. Having studied German at Istanbul University and later in Berlin, he became one of the most productive and influential translators of German fiction, drama and poetry, and is credited with over 30 titles, including Scandinavian ones rendered from the German. His translation of Rilke's *The Notes of Malte Laurids Brigge* reputedly became an indispensable companion to the younger generation of Turkish poets, and a posthumous collection of his translations of German and Austrian poetry was published in 1984. Necatigil also translated and produced radio plays of his own (collected in four volumes from 1965 onward), in which he freed his imagination to roam over a variety of themes that often resonated with his poems, such as the mysteries of female-male relationships and traditional myths, as in 'The Three Oranges', an excerpt from which appears in this issue. It illustrates the background of the 20th century zeitgeist in Turkey as his other plays also do.

Behçet Necatigil centenary celebrations took place on April 13th and 14th, 2016, and included a major symposium in his memory held at the Mimar Sinan University of Fine Arts, Istanbul, which was attended by his poet friends, colleagues, former students, and literary critics. In addition, during their September 2015 session members of the Cunda International Workshop for Translators of Turkish Literature focused on translating his poetry, radio plays and essays, thereby producing the first major selection of Behçet Necatigil's work in English.

The Editors

Beşiktaş-Ortaköy

How pleasant morning and evening
To walk on the same sidewalk
With the road stretching ahead
At the foot of a high wall.

On the one side lamp posts
On the other the wall
Not jolly not worried
Unconcerned as a stone

No trace of friends
No heart's desire
Tranquil, alone
I tread the path.

What bliss it is to journey
As far as school from home
Leaving along the road
A clutch of memories

Careful as I traverse them
Not to disturb the long
Narrow sun-baked
Cracked sidewalks.

Who knows how much longer
I'll need to walk this way
At the foot of a high
Long and barren wall.

Translated by Clifford Endres and Selhan Savcıgil Endres

'Beşiktaş-Ortaköy' from Necatigil, Behçet. *Şiirler: Bütün Yapıtları*. Istanbul: Yapı Kredi Yayınları, 2014. (*Varlık* 67, April 15, 1936)

School days at Kabataş Lisesi, May 27, 1933

Cowboy Movies

I'm off to a cheap movie
When I've got the one or two bits
They want for seats.

Cowboy movies always rope me in:
Forget the girl,
The leads are men.
Songs, music, fuss and din
Fists, fights, bullets and guns;
Hooray, yay, hit, crack
Bedlam reigns throughout the salon.

Scenes are simplistic, sure
Graceless? Let them be then!
The bad guys have to pay in the end
Justice rules, that's it, my friend!

Fair play and a straightshooter's sense
Are what cowboy films dispense.

Translated by Mel Kenne and Arzu Eker Roditakis

Kovboy Filmleri

Ucuz sinemalara giderim,
Cebimde fazla para oldukta
Otururum koltukta.

Kovboy filmlerine biterim:
Kızı hesaba katma,
Artistler yalnız erkek.
Şarkı, çalgı, gürültü
Kavga, yumruk, tabanca
Yaşa, vur, kır sesleri
Çın çın öter salonda.

Sahneler basitmiş, basit
İncelik yokmuş, yok!
Kötüler ceza yer en sonda
Adalet var, iş onda!

Hak hukuk dağıtma yeri
Kovboy filmleri.

'Kovboy Filmleri' from *Kapalı Çarşı*. Necatigil, Behçet. *Şiirler: Bütün Yapıtları.* Istanbul: Yapı Kredi Yayınları, 2014. (*Kovan*, 21, Nisan 1945)

The Shame of a Dead Man

Never could I turn my hand to anything,
I lived my life to no benefit.
I would not have survived, I would have died
If it were not for you.

So many of you went to great lengths for me,
I was a burden on your back, truly.
And now I need your help once more
If it's no trouble, for the last time.

Just as you brought my wood from the forest,
And as you baked my dough in your oven,
Please just lay me in my grave
As you see fit.

Translated by Caroline Stockford

'Ölü Utanıyor' from *Çevre*. Necatigil, Behçet. *Şiirler: Bütün Yapıtları*. Istanbul: Yapı Kredi Yayınları, 2014. (*Yirminci Asır*, 1, 20 January 1947)

As Long as Fires Burn in the Mountains

The room is dark
Leave the room
The city is dark
Leave the city
Don't be afraid
Walk on, walk for a while
Do you see
Now the mountains begin

Your fear melts away in the wind
Wait for a moment
As long as fires burn in the mountains
Darkness need not be feared

The mountains are dark
Don't be afraid
To go into the mountains
Walk on, walk for a while
Go on up a bit higher
Do you see how,
Far apart from each other,
The fires are glowing now.

Now the mountains are again left behind.
Your room has conquered darkness and death
As long as fires burn in the mountains
Darkness need not be feared, don't you see?

Translated by Mel Kenne and İdil Karacadağ

'Dağlarda Ateşler Yandıkça' from *Çevre*. Necatigil, Behçet. *Şiirler: Bütün Yapıtları*. Istanbul: Yapı Kredi Yayınları, 2014. (*Yeditepe*, 4, 15 May 1950)

Sleepless Night Quatrains

On that insufferable night
Sleep had fled
I wrote poetry
Nearing daybreak.

A story? No!
Maybe one in fragments
Disconnected memories
Coming together.

A village, my feet cut by stubble
Then I was taken to the cities.
When a child's left motherless
All's over and done with.

A girl, growing up for bars,
This very moment senses the man.
On her white breast dirty
Bread for home.

A seed, could it find no other path
Brink of an abyss, a breast bared for floods.
How come she couldn't see this coming,
The fate of other saplings, so obvious.

You, lived for as long as you could,
Were wiped out, gone, like a shadow.
No need for 'like',
In photos you are a shadow now.

A loved one, wouldn't heed her family,
Believed in you, came to wed you.
You would feel some warmth
In your hands, wouldn't you?

A wound, often stretches out over years
Tossing up the earth like moles a bit here,
A bit there, burrowing down below,
Mounds that turn green after the rain.

A woman, in Eve's bed
Just when the moon entered the cloud,
Just there, of fantasies
Three dots or a dash.

Thought, lives on in human beings
For centuries, whatever the thought may be
Despite all that happens
Doesn't die, let them kill it if they can.

Poetry, eleven quatrains, each one different
I knew it would turn out this way,
Didn't I say at the start
I'm sleepless.

Translated by Saliha Paker and Mel Kenne

'Uykusuz Gecede Dörtlükler' from *Çevre*. Necatigil, Behçet. *Şiirler: Bütün Yapıtları*. Istanbul: Yapı Kredi Yayınları, 2014.(*Yeni Şiirler*, Varlık Yayınlerı, 1954.)

The Bow

Sounds well up from the deep
Not even your love can help
Wait until it passes
Don't strain the bow much tighter
You'll snap it.

The eye within you cannot see
The crawling thought in the dark
In this moment when I'm swathed in layers
The cloths have fallen from you
You are naked

A cool breeze is blowing
You are all heat
My hands slipped from you, the bridge gave way
How can I bring you to my side?
You are distant.

Translated by Caroline Stockford

'Yay' from *Eski Toprak*. Necatigil, Behçet. *Şiirler: Bütün Yapıtları*. Istanbul: Yapı Kredi Yayınları, 2014. (*Varlık*, 396, 1 July 1953)

Cross

Trains, Boats, Stars…
I'd like to invest my money in travel,
To live in distant cities…But where?
Rent, electricity, water bills
The butcher, the grocer, the tailor…
I close out one, a new one opens
Doors of expenses, a fantasy doorway

Trains, Boats, Stars…
I'd like to spend my life on the road.
Yet it's doled out among homes.
And everyone's after the lion's share:
A father, a mother, a sibling
Each one left forlorn without me.
From aunts and uncles on both sides, a plea:
Don't forget us!
From spouses, children, that sad, sorry look:
You're only Ours!

We work right on into the evening.
Sometimes deep into the night too.
On trains, on boats, to take off, go far away
And live all alone... But where?
Money tossed to the wind, a life doled out
Our lot? only this, some place in-between.

Translated by Mel Kenne and İdil Karacadağ

'Çarmıh' from *Eski Toprak*. Necatigil, Behçet. *Şiirler: Bütün Yapıtları*. Istanbul: Yapı Kredi Yayınları, 2014.(*Yeni Şiirler*, Varlık Yayınları, 1954)

What We Have On

While I live in darkness
You too dress in black...
Wear blues, tomorrow morning,
come from the sea.

Fresh grass, bright weeds, flowers
pink, green, ultramarine.
Young women, tender girls, I don't want them
to wear black.
No-one wear it.

Translated by Caroline Stockford

Üstümüzdeki

Ben karalarda yaşarken
Bir de sende siyah…
Maviler giy gel denizden
Yarın sabah.

Taze çimen, parlak ot, çiçek
Pembe, yeşil, tirşe.
Genç kadınlar, körpe kızlar, istemem
Giymesinler siyah
Giymesin kimse.

'Üstümüzdeki' from *Eski Toprak*. Necatigil, Behçet. *Şiirler: Bütün Yapıtları*. Istanbul: Yapı Kredi Yayınları, 2014. (*Yenilik*, 8, August 1954)

Literary Matinée

Leaning back in her chair a girl
Chewing gum.
A boy monkeying around,
Another one behind dozes off,
Sorry he's there.

Could the bird you let fly
Find the white house far away?
The snowy mountain sharp as a sword.
Under this hard light, is this really the place
To open up the heart.

Before you, someone read a fantasy
Bringing down the house.
From broad smiles mouths return very late;
Now sad, heavy, your turn comes around
How nice!

If only a few here
Were uneasy, with similar feelings,
Having been there too.
You under the light, they indiscernible,
All in the dark.

You have read,
Happy it's over,
And with nothing understood;
Before you, like loose change
The applause falls

There on the ground
Mushed like rotten tomatoes
You see your heart battered between palms.
As the stain spread on fine silk
You bowed and bowed!

Translated by Nilgün Dungan and Mel Kenne

'Edebiyat Matinesi' from *Eski Toprak*. Necatigil, Behçet. *Şiirler: Bütün Yapıtları*. Istanbul: Yapı Kredi Yayınları, 2014. (*Yenilik*, 28, April 1955)

Blood

Within sheaths and layers, blood cannot be seen
A pink wave on rose cheeks
A blue ribbon on snow-white hands
Red blood cells suddenly drop
In blind wells, lost

Family traits passed on in white milk
Greed hides for years in a generous soul
Ugliness in the skin-tight shirt of a beauty
Imposes itself on a coming generation.
Blood can't be seen buried under the skin.

The murderer, psychopath, the epileptic
Wakes, having slipped into transient sleep.
A dirty drop seeping from far-distant breasts
A poor soul still in childhood
Suffers sins of faces he's never seen

Year upon year a friend hides his enmity
Pus building up within
Releasing its familiar voice through us alone
The buried link in the chain of genes
Awakes, slyness of the deep exposed

Blue or red
Leaks down from deaths
Arriving in strange feelings
A so-distant relative lives in our body
Suckles the same hope as us in our sleep

Suddenly a thin vein is blocked by a blood clot
One always cheerful, never seen to be sad
Hears from a secret voice hushed in his artery
The awful news that toppled his grandfather
And collapses whilst walking the street

Ferhat and Kerem walk towards a mirage
Their legs are tired, the road is long
Thirsty for Şirin, hungry for Aslı
They are united, is that the lot?
Blood pushes, it is weary.
Held back by shame, pride and fear
On the outside people veil what they say
topped with foam
Blood
Says everything
Openly.

Eve lives on in blood from girls and women
In guns and knives
Cain
Lives on

Tomato carnation cherry blood
Sun fire coral winter summer blood
Humankind earth water air
First there was blood
Only later
Came white

Translated by Caroline Stockford and Arzu Eker Roditakis

'Kan' from *Eski Toprak*. Necatigil, Behçet. *Şiirler: Bütün Yapıtları*. Istanbul: Yapı Kredi Yayınları, 2014. (*Varlık*, 418, 1 May 1955)

The Milky Way

I should have been much taller
Then, while walking side by side on a summer night
With your head against my chest
As you looked up at my face and smiled
I could have taken a handful of stars from the sky
And sprinkled them on your hair.

Translated by Arzu Eker Roditakis

'Samanyolu' from Necatigil, Behçet. *Şiirler: Bütün Yapıtları*. Istanbul: Yapı Kredi Yayınları, 2014.

The Waters of Heraclitus

Whenever I wander the streets
Schools cinemas shop fronts
Each use up
The old me's in me.

In crowds I multiply
Unsure of which self I'll reach
The image of her features
That woman across the street.

This small child
The me of many years ago
Would he be scared if I tipped up to him
To say, ah child you are me.

Three young men out walking
Each at the head of a crossroads
And I split in three
Down each road goes one of me.

One to his studies, I am opening a book
One a lover, I am waiting in the park
The third works somewhere after school
At this late hour of the night, I am heading home.

Hey stop, I say, you are me
But where are you going without me, hey stop
They just keep walking in silence oblivious of me
And refuse to hear no matter how loud I call out.

Translated by Neil P. Doherty

'Heraklit'in Suları' from *Arada*. Necatigil, Behçet. *Şiirler: Bütün Yapıtları*, Istanbul: Yapı Kredi Yayınları, 2014. (*Varlık*, 486, 15 September 1958)

Bone

And into the ceilings seeps a smell of tallow
From the candles so quietly quenched
And people looking right looking left
In haste bury something so nobody sees at all
And then down the long boulevard they run

And at night from the flocks a sheep goes missing
And people looking right looking left pass
In haste cross over one last time before they die
Then later in solitude they sit and lick
A very old bone they'd plucked from the walls.

Translated by Neil P. Doherty

Kemik

Ve siner tavanlara bir iç yağı kokusu
Sessizce söndürülen mumlardan
Ve insanlar gömerler sağa sola bakınıp
Çok acele bir şeyi görmeden kimsecikler
Ve sonra koşarlar upuzun bulvarlardan

Ve eksilir bir koyun geceye davarlardan
Ve insanlar geçerler sağa sola bakınıp
Çok acele bir şeyi ölmeden bir kez daha
Sonra yalnızlıklarda otururlar yalarlar
Çok eski bir kemiği çıkarıp duvarlardan.

'Kemik' from *Yaz Dönemi*. Necatigil, Behçet. *Şiirler: Bütün Yapıtları*. Istanbul: Yapı Kredi Yayınları, 2014. (*Varlık*, 560, 15 January 1961)

Panther

In the forests a roe deer
& there lying in wait, the panther of life.
Fleeing, out of breath
To some secret attic.

The booksteps lead even further up:
The tiny sky I freed from the hugest buildings!
Over my soil pour all of your mercy
At night mostly come the pleas.

Should I slightly open this one blind left shut for years
So that onto your pale face will fall
A morning of flowers from my most distant poems;
But are you yet again a roe deer in the forests
And I, still up against those days?

Translated by Neil P. Doherty

'Pars' from *Yaz Dönemi*. Necatigil, Behçet. *Şiirler: Bütün Yapıtları*, Istanbul: Yapı Kredi Yayınları, 2014. (*Varlık*, 560, 15 January 1961)

The Flowers of Fear

No flowers of the prophet -
It was always flowers of fear
That graced our pots.

From the skies that we stared at frightened and jaded
Hope in tomorrow is all we ever asked
Children, homes and bread…
But happiness, is this all there is?

Should a seed green in a poisonous ground
From the hemlock it has drunk blooms
A flower of fear, a corrupted crop.
It needs to be grafted, it needs to be cut
But isn't it too late for us.

Every line we reached became a wall
When we couldn't scale the slippery moss
And what comes next you know well
The world is beautiful…
If in it you don't dwell.

Translated by Neil P. Doherty

'Korku Çiçekleri' from *Divançe*. Necatigil, Behçet. *Şiirler: Bütün Yapıtları*, Istanbul: Yapı Kredi Yayınları, 2014. (*Varlık*, 562, November 1961)

A Pale Rose When I Touch

Many like her end up here yet no passer-by cares
I bend down and pick her up
She becomes a pale rose when I touch

Wandering in one of those big cities
Among the crowd at bus stops
Or in a far-off corner of the country, in a café or in a hotel
Wherever she goes at these late hours
She hides her hands in her pockets
Flowing slowly among the cigarettes and papers
I bend down and pick her up, she becomes no one
But a pale rose when I touch

Or in the wiped off lipstick of a lonesome girl
As she rests her head on the pillows
On the edge of the weary night

Sometimes even in the middle of the day she sidles up
Mostly in fall you know when a cloud descends
and it rains, in that cloud of sorrow
I reach out and pick her up, she becomes no one
But a pale rose when I touch

In hands, between the lips, in wild scripts
She is caught by the night nets
panting like a wounded animal
smothered, wanting to flee
Through the roads through memories
Again and again I bring her back, all night she lies awake,
Tosses and turns in the dark and becomes
A pale rose when I touch.

Translated by Gökçenur Ç & Neil P. Doherty

'Solgun Bir Gül Dokununca' from *Yaz Dönemi*. Necatigil, Behçet. *Şiirler: Bütün Yapıtları*, Istanbul: Yapı Kredi Yayınları, 2014. (*Varlık*, 565, January 1962)

A Feeling for Love

Stretched out over ivory keys
In a room with the curtains drawn
Impulsive, tense, practiced fingers
And play out hcr girlhood, dolcndo.

This is the sound you suddenly hear in the night.

She knew she would always be in her own world,
And she hadn't seen everything.
But how did she feel it? She felt it
And take away her loneliness, dolendo.

This is the tear that suddenly spills in the night.

Translated by John Angliss

'Aşk Duyarlığı' from *Yaz Dönemi*, Necatigil, Behçet. *Şiirler: Bütün Yapıtları*. Istanbul: Yapı Krcdi Yayınları, 2014. (*Ataç*, 2, 15 June 1962)

The Water Lily

I had put it there they took it away
There between the crammed hours
I'd take it out to look when no one was around
It was the mirror that would show me to myself,
They took it away.

Spring in winter, blossoming in my waters
What need to smuggle it behind the icy mountains?
A leaf yellowed in an old notebook.
It was the meaning that would show me to myself,
They took it away.

It was a light that burned only at night;
Evening, the flowers lie down to sleep
Darkness enfolding the shore across -
It was the lamp that would show me to myself,
They took it away.

Translated by Gökçenur Ç and Neil P. Doherty

'Nilüfer' from *Yaz Dönemi*. Necatigil, Behçet. *Şiirler: Bütün Yapıtları*, Istanbul: Yapı Kredi Yayınları, 2014. (*Türk Dili*, 139, 1 April 1963)

Winter Shopping Net

Say, on your way - write it down - don't forget
Oranges, cheese and meat.
How tiny this park how sparse its green
Trampled by hurrying feet.

Villages but which of the villages
How tiny this park in its squat flowerpots
The poor idyll of cramped houses
Ah Arcadia forever lost!

What post is this boat - fine, so farewell
Who is this man staring out at dusty streets -
For the longest time I have loved rhyme
Oranges, cheese and meat.

Translated by Neil P. Doherty

'Kış Filesi' from *Divançe*. Necatigil, Behçet. *Şiirler: Bütün Yapıtları*, Istanbul: Yapı Kredi Yayınları, 2014. (*Yeni Dergi*, 9, June 1965)

Bed

Somewhere everything is like the last days of Pompeii -
We are as we were when the lava was poured over us.
As for clothes strip & discard those old ones.

There so far away - fallen behind
He thinks: who are they who came & took
My coarse old clothes
To dress me in coarser ones still.

Sleeping so long on the mattress they laid down
That looked so different then,
But was really always the same.

Perhaps once it was some lovely, ever changing pattern -
As childhood restores the old glass cabinets...
No matter how much they turn its face it still
Falls behind.

Translated by Neil P. Doherty

'Yatak' from *İki Başına Yürümek*. Necatigil, Behçet. *Şiirler: Bütün Yapıtları*, Istanbul: Yapı Kredi Yayınları, 2014. (*Yeni Dergi*, 29, February 1967)

Harbour

Their masts wrecked in heavy storms, the ships come &
Take refuge in us - we think we have found them.

They see nothing but the far distances.
We mend them - they go & we stay.

Then, at night- let this be the last, the last,
Send no more - we beg of the sea.

And then our loneliness grows
 - more terrible still.

Translated by Neil P. Doherty

'Liman' from *İki Başına Yürümek*. Necatigil, Behçet. *Şiirler: Bütün Yapıtları*, Istanbul: Yapı Kredi Yayınları, 2014. (*Yeni Dergi*, 42, March 1968)

Text

And for whom do the poets always write?
If at the edge of bridges ruined
Someone howls in a terrified abyss
And for those 'I am heres' do the poets always write.

Translated by Gökçenur Ç & Neil P. Doherty

Yazı

Ve şairler boyuna kimlere yazarlar?
Yıkılmış köprülerin başında
Ürkmüş boşluktan biri inliyor
Ve şairler onlara geldimlere yazarlar.

'Yazı' from *En / Cam*. Necatigil, Behçet. *Şiirler: Bütün Yapıtları*, Istanbul: Yapı Kredi Yayınları, 2014. (*Yeni Dergi*, 61, October 1969)

Zebra

Do not trip over
Each trivial example
A typical resistance.

Though buried - it still flies
Duped perching on a branch by times
The migratory bird bound for eternity.

Zebra!
Wander from circus to circus
For I arise - & you, are risen?

A reciprocated lull lullaby
In this palace even the kings are slaves
& othello, a mere hotel.

Translated by Neil P. Doherty

'Zebra' from *Zebra*. Necatigil, Behçet. *Şiirler: Bütün Yapıtları*, Istanbul: Yapı Kredi Yayınları, 2014. (*Cumhuriyet, Sanat-Edibiyat Eki*, September 1970)

Inheritance

Much melon eaten & much white cheese
Much drink drunk
Much disgrace suffered.

Forgotten how it was but still pricked by thought
You are dead to me, they say, love was taken away
But who has waxed here & who has waned there.

Pain in short all purified
How many shutters seized shut, fields sowed in vengeance
And reaped just for us.

Translated by Gökçenur Ç & Neil P. Doherty

'Kalıt' from *Zebra*. Necatigil, Behçet. *Şiirler: Bütün Yapıtları*, Istanbul: Yapı Kredi Yayınları, 2014. (*Yeni Dergi*, 95, August 1972)

Bulldozer

It's a common police action
Kids and grown-ups -
A flattened house,
A bulldozer.

What time was it, oh, five or six in the morning
What was it, oh, a flash like a red-winged bird
But they saw it
The massive lightness of a bulldozer.

Translated by Clifford Endres and Selhan Savcıgil Endres

Buldozer

Adi bir zabıta olayı
Büyükler, bebeler -
Bir evi yere serdi
Bir buldozer.

Saat kaçtı beş altı öyle bir şey
Bir kuş al kanatlı öyle bir şey
Ama görmüşlerdi
Hafif ağır bir buldozer.

'Buldozer' from *Kareler Aklar*. Necatigil, Behçet. *Şiirler: Bütün Yapıtları*, Istanbul: Yapı Kredi Yayınları, 2014. (*Yeni Dergi*, 112, January 1974)

Filigree

Some papers
If you hold them to light:
a line, a picture, a figure.
Or written in invisible ink
A seemingly blank page
Is read when held closer to heat.

Some poems
Are better read if behind them
Is a burning of your own.

Translated by Nilgün Dungan

Filigran

Kimi kâğıtlar
Aydınlığa tutsanız
Çizgi, resim, bir şekil.
Ya da gizli mürekkeple yazılmış
Boş görünen sayfa
Okunur ısıya yaklaştırınca.

Kimi şiirler
Okunur arkasında
Kendi ateşiniz varsa.

'Filigran' from *Beyler*. Necatigil, Behçet. *Şiirler: Bütün Yapıtları*, Istanbul: Yapı Kredi Yayınları, 2014. (*Varlık, 841*, October 1977)

[A joy to see so many of us poets]

A joy to see so many of us
Poets named in the yearly summary

To see how a poem or a journey
Can discharge the poison within us.

This thin string can lift
Much heaviness, propped by
Other strings unseen.

Most go on talking
Like machine-gun fire
We keep pausing
Even in wars.

Translated by Saliha Paker and Arzu Eker Roditakis

[Ne çok şairmişiz sevindim] from Necatigil, Behçet. *Şiirler: Bütün Yapıtları*, Istanbul: Yapı Kredi Yayınları, 2014.

From an Istanbullu's Notebook I

It's no different from when
I was a child -
Still relying on a candle
When the electricity winks out.

Sloshing through muck and slush all winter
As in my old school days -
Thank God for two feet to walk on
When I can't find a ride.

Street after street on the appointed days
Thank God for mobile bazaars -
I can still hunt for good bargains
At my grandmother's old haunts.

Slush, candles, bazaars
Richocheting from one to the next
Is what's made me tough.

Brushed aside by boorish cars
Wary of being crushed at the drop of a hat
I've become this old dodderer.

Somebody wrote it
In a book somewhere
I'm what he wrote.

Translated by Clifford Endres and Selhan Savcıgil Endres

'Bir İstanbullu'nun Not Defterinden I' from *Söyleriz*. Necatigil, Behçet. *Şiirler: Bütün Yapıtları*, Istanbul: Yapı Kredi Yayınları, 2014. (*Varlık, 857*, February 1979)

From an Istanbullu's Notebook II

On the streets the faces of our reality
Park in their hundreds on the sidewalks
Just one car-free road please
We struggle in vain to find.

Wave down a vehicle and beg
Climb in whatever it takes
Foot on the gas a driver zooms by
Bathing me in a fountain of mud.

As crowds from hell push and shove
I withdraw farther into my corner
After all I'm a man of many years
Where else can I go?

If I should ask when the bus
Is due at this stop
They laugh at me and say
Wait a while, Pops, just wait.

And all winter, summer, and fall I wait
In queues curling like a dog's tail
It's in Istanbul that I live
If you call that living.

Translated by Clifford Endres and Selhan Savcıgil Endres

'Bir İstanbullu'nun Not Defterinden II' from *Söyleriz*. Necatigil, Behçet. *Şiirler: Bütün Yapıtları*, Istanbul: Yapı Kredi Yayınları, 2014 (*Varlık, 859,* April 1979)

From an Istanbullu's Notebook III

One of them sent me to the next
He's a doctor, he ought to know
This is not your only sickness
No, it wasn't.

A third doctor was called in
And yet a few others like me
Saw no doctors at all
Should they have?

Translated by Clifford Endres and Selhan Savcıgil Endres

Bir İstanbullu'nun Not Defterinden III

Beni biri ötekine yolladı
Doktordu, bilirdi
Hastalığınız yalnız bu değil,
Değildi.

Üçüncü bir doktora ihtiyaç belirdi
Benim gibi bazıları
Hiç doktora gitmedi
Gitseler miydi?

'Bir İstanbullu'nun Not Defterinden III' from *Söyleriz*. Necatigil, Behçet. *Şiirler: Bütün Yapıtları*, Istanbul: Yapı Kredi Yayınları, 2014. (*Varlık, 862*, July 1979)

[We've been there too, does that matter]

We've been there too, does that matter
Our poems too were translated
Into the languages of the West.

Unless a Western reader
Has passed down those lines that I have
How well could he understand me
A Zebra in the circus.

If he reads me
In search of amusement
I'd rather not have that benefit
No!

If, to my own countrymen
I can't explain what I want to say,
I'd rather do without the West
Better let it rest!

Translated by Saliha Paker

[Biz de gittik önemli mi] from *Söyleriz*. Necatigil, Behçet. *Şiirler: Bütün Yapıtları*, Istanbul: Yapı Kredi Yayınları, 2014.*Başlık Konulmamış Şiirler*, 1980

Not a stir in the mind

Not a stir in in the mind
Pain must have put memories to flight
Like a mother saving her child

Translated by Nilgün Dungan

'Çıt yok bellekte' from Necatigil, Behçet. *Şiirler: Bütün Yapıtları*, Istanbul: Yapı Kredi Yayınları, 2014. (*Günümüzde Kitaplar*, 12, December 1984)

The Three Oranges

Seeing that my love for the Three Oranges
Was becoming inescapable
Giddy up, I said hopping onto my horse
What the prince did, so did I

A mansion facing a fountain
From one tap flows blood, from the other pus
I drank from both nozzles of the fountain
When I did

A lion, in front of the lion hay
A horse, in front of the horse meat
Gave hay to the horse, meat to the lion
When I did

Before me appeared two doors
One wide open
One closed for years
Closed the open one,
Opened the closed one
When I did

The Sultan's Garden
Hanging there the Three Oranges
Took all three
Whipped up my horse

Up to now
A snap
Then came twists and turns
How shapeless my path became
In mid-desert.

On and on I went
Cut one of the oranges
Water my prince, water please

But where was the water?

Drenched in sweat
Through deserts
I'll cut the second one, I said
When I come across some water.

On and on I went
A puddle
Left from the rain
Cut the second orange
Water my prince, water please
Her lips, as they almost touched it
The water vanished.
A worry ties your hands
It's no secret without water, it can't work
In tales the prince
Fulfilled his desire but
First he found his water.

Translated by Nilgun Dungan and Mel Kenne

'Üç Turunçlar' from *Çevre*. Necatigil, Behçet. *Şiirler: Bütün Yapıtları*, Istanbul: Yapı Kredi Yayınları, 2014. (*Varlık*, 363, 1 October 1950) *from* 'The Three Oranges', a Radio Play

[...]

DIRECTOR: (*Scolding*) Do not interrupt me. Okay, you ignored both me and the writer. What about the audience? What would they say?
PRODUCER: I'm sure they will like it. Besides, the play is easier to understand this way.
DIRECTOR: What if it becomes completely impossible to understand? So that's it, huh? I congratulate you on your new position!
PRODUCER: (*Silent*)
DIRECTOR: Director and assistant writer Mr. Producer!
PRODUCER: (*Offended*) You're mocking me!
DIRECTOR: (*Angry*) I will not let this play be aired. I will also make a complaint against you, you'll be held responsible. This play cannot be aired like this tonight!
PRODUCER: (*Alarmed*) But...it's been announced already, we will lose face. We can't possibly find another play for the program this late.
DIRECTOR: Well, who will lose face if it's aired? Me and the writer! Nothing in it for you!
PRODUCER: (*Imploring*) Mr. Director, please listen to it and then say so if you don't like it.
DIRECTOR: (*Softens up*) Alright, let's listen to it then! We'll see! Everybody should mind their own business, my friend, everybody should mind... (*Quick silence; the voice machine begins to roll.*)
NARRATOR: One day an old hag arrived at the fountain with two jugs. She filled one jug with butter, the other with honey. Just as she was about to put them on her shoulders and leave, the sultan's son threw rocks at the jugs, breaking both of them. What could the old hag do? So she placed a curse on the prince...

(*The button is pushed; the sound is cut off immediately*)

DIRECTOR: (*Angry*) Give me my play back. It's turned into a tale, this is too much!
PRODUCER: Not a single sentence is omitted from the play. Just a little patience, please!

(*The machine resumes playing.*)

(*The YOUNG MAN and the YOUNGEST SISTER are inside a car.*)

YOUNG MAN: This bloody old man of mine...
YOUNGEST SISTER: Your father?
YOUNG MAN: My father! He started fussing now. All he gives is a pittance anyway, and he's even reluctant to do that without complaining about it.
YOUNGEST SISTER: Then get a job!
YOUNG MAN: It's too early. What is this! I will work, why the hurry? He says: I spent everything I had for you... Check this out: He says he's spent my weight in money and I didn't amount to anything!... How much do I weigh anyway?
YOUNGEST SISTER: How much?
YOUNG MAN: Well, who else would know it better? Haven't you felt my weight enough?
YOUNGEST SISTER: My lion!
YOUNG MAN: Damn right! Are you up for the bar?
YOUNGEST SISTER: Sure thing, let's go.
YOUNG MAN: No leaving early though.
YOUNGEST SISTER: No.
YOUNG MAN: Your folks?
YOUNGEST SISTER: The hell with the shack! I'm dying in this heat. Five people! Three girls in one tiny room.
YOUNG MAN: You're the most beautiful one!
NARRATOR: The old hag cursed the boy, you will fall in love with the Three Oranges, she said! Before long he set his mind on the Three Oranges. He then set out on a long troublesome journey. On and on he walked! Then he met a giantess, hugging her immediately, he suckled on her breasts. 'Oh dear Mother!' he said. She replied, 'If you hadn't called me mother, I would have eaten you right away, away away'.

(*After a brief sputter, the tape stops.*)

DIRECTOR: It's like a broken record. What is this now?
PRODUCER: A small malfunction. It'll be alright in a minute... Okay!

(*The machine resumes.*)

YOUNG MAN: How many times have I told you this: Come with me, be my lover. We can rent a room. Run away from that shack! You're beautiful, your sisters aren't!
YOUNGEST SISTER: (*Giggling*) Don't let them hear it.
YOUNG MAN: Isn't that right, though? Each one is more wretched than the other.
YOUNGEST SISTER: My older sister is on to us. She tells me not to talk to you. If only she knew I go out with you!
YOUNG MAN: Ignore her! If your mother doesn't say anything, why does she care? Look how I won your mother's heart. I know how to play the game. I sometimes go to your house when your sisters are at work. A little sweet talk and a few strokes on her chin, she becomes putty in my hands. Like she doesn't know we are lovers anyway.
YOUNGEST SISTER: But she's afraid my sisters will find out.
YOUNG MAN: Never mind that! You're not a child.
YOUNGEST SISTER: I'm not.
YOUNG MAN: Your mother knows.
YOUNGEST SISTER: She does.
YOUNG MAN: Are you going to rot away like them?
YOUNGEST SISTER: I've had enough...
YOUNG MAN: Oh, we're here. (*Raises his voice.*) Hey driver, let us out here, won't you? (*The taxi brakes and stops.*)
NARRATOR: The boy told the giantess he was looking for the Three Oranges. The giantess told him: 'Go here and here, follow this path, like so and so, go on and on! A mansion will appear before you. In front of the mansion is a fountain with two taps. Blood flows from one, pus from the other...'
YOUNG MAN: We're here.
YOUNGEST SISTER: What a horrible place.
YOUNG MAN: Horrible? It's a bar. Look at its gate!
YOUNGEST SISTER: A tap on both the left and the right.
YOUNG MAN: (*Laughs*) They're not taps.
YOUNGEST SISTER: Then what are they?
YOUNG MAN: Ornaments.
YOUNGEST SISTER: What's in them?
YOUNG MAN: Nothing...Two light bulbs.
YOUNGEST SISTER: One is yellow, like pus.
YOUNG MAN: The other's red.

YOUNGEST SISTER: The color of blood.
YOUNG MAN: Blood flows often here. People get inside each other's head...Give me your hand, let's get inside...

(*A door opens and closes. The button is pushed, the voice machine stops.*)

PRODUCER: This scene, it matches the tale, doesn't it?
DIRECTOR: (*Smiles softly*) Not bad, the rate you're going, you'll be writing better plays than our famous writer!
PRODUCER: You're flattering me.
DIRECTOR: Go on, go on!

(*The voice machine resumes.*)

NARRATOR: The giantess told her son: 'Drink some of that blood and some of that pus! Then you'll see a dog, there's hay in front of it. And you'll see a horse, there's some meat in front of it. Give the hay to the horse and the meat to the dog!'

(*A brief silence. Bar music. The YOUNGEST SISTER and the YOUNG MAN are drunk.*)

YOUNGEST SISTER: Oh my, how bright is this! I'm dazzled.
YOUNG MAN: Close your eyes!
YOUNGEST SISTER: I've seen it only in movies. We don't turn on the lights at home.
YOUNG MAN: Your eyes are almost closed; you're very beautiful!
YOUNGEST SISTER: There are so many lights in the local coffee-house. Each time I pass by it, I want to count them but I never can... there are that many...' What if my folks woke up? They'll know it.
YOUNG MAN: We've decided. There's no more going back home.
YOUNGEST SISTER: (*Laughs*) Oh, how's that possible, sweetie?
YOUNG MAN: We'll live together. You're not little!
YOUNGEST SISTER: I'm not.
YOUNG MAN: No one can say a thing. Not your mother, not your father, nor your sisters!
YOUNGEST SISTER: My mother won't. She's anxious to get rid of me.
YOUNG MAN: If you wanted...my God! You'd better want it!
YOUNGEST SISTER: I do, but what if you leave me in the end? I'll

be walking the streets. (*She laughs.*)

YOUNG MAN: I said I'm smitten, That's enough…Your arms are white as snow!

YOUNGEST SISTER: (*Laughs*) No one takes me to the beach!

YOUNG MAN: We'll go to beaches, how nice is that! We'll rent a room…that's it! Then get married in the future! What more do you want! Your mother's only too pleased. If we give her some dough, she'll handle your father, too.

(*The YOUNGEST SISTER laughs.*)

YOUNG MAN: Girl, move those legs of yours, I feel faint!

YOUNGEST SISTER: (*Flirting*) Then do! (*She laughs.*) Look, a photographer… Come on let's get our picture taken together!

YOUNG MAN: Your wish is my command, my darling! (*He hollers.*) Photo!

NARRATOR: The giantess continued: 'You'll see two doors, one open, one closed… Close the open door, open the closed one! Walk through the door you opened, have no fear, go upstairs! There the Three Oranges are hanging. Don't be afraid to pick them, then come back without even looking back!'

YOUNG MAN: Never mind them. We're young! I mean aren't you young? This stuff takes courage, my friend! Enjoy it while it's ripe. These cherries, these peaches, these oranges… You know what I mean, right? (*He laughs.*)

DIRECTOR: Stop it!

(*The button is pushed, the recording stops.*)

PRODUCER: What is it?

DIRECTOR: He said oranges.

PRODUCER: Yes?

DIRECTOR: Now I see how you connected it with the tale. Bravo! It actually matches the play.

PRODUCER: Thank you.

DIRECTOR: Go on!

(*The voice machine continues.*)

YOUNG MAN: ...these oranges... You know what I mean, right! (*He laughs.*)

YOUNGEST SISTER: I do. (*She laughs.*)

YOUNG MAN: Look, we've gone out quite a few times. Went to the movies, ice cream parlors. We ate corn together...wafers, chocolate, soda.. Has your father bought you anything like those?

YOUNGEST SISTER: You must be joking!

YOUNG MAN: But I got more... Look, I even brought you to a bar... You're worth it... See, because of you I even ignore my father... He wants me married... And with a girl of high order.

YOUNGEST SISTER: (*Laughs.*) A girl of high order? What exactly is that?

YOUNG MAN: I mean, darling...never mind, she's no good. Nothing like you. I fiddled around once or twice, she didn't even pay attention. The fool curled her lip... You're different... You're the most beautiful. Why don't you drink some more!

YOUNGEST SISTER: I feel dizzy. Let's go already.

YOUNG MAN: We will. Now straight to my house. The old man left the house to me tonight. You didn't dance here... At home, we'll put something on the record player, then let the dancing begin! We have cognac, too. Leave it to me. At any rate, I'll take you to your house early in the morning; no one will be any the wiser.

YOUNGEST SISTER: I'm scared. (*She laughs.*)

YOUNG MAN: Nonsense! There are two rooms. You can stay in my father's... Lock the door if you want. But if you say...well, that's different. No lies, you understand? We'll go, open the door; I have the key... We'll have some fun at home, too... Besides, it'll be a change for you. So what happens? Are you going to waste your youth in that shack? Let's live the life, for god's sake! Now there isn't a soul in sight in the streets. We'll turn on the record player, play gently, and let the dancing begin! Then we'll go to bed and sleep... In the morning, you're at your home, okay... (*Hurt*) I'll get a job, work, we'll get married... what more do you want?

YOUNGEST SISTER: What if they hear about it?

YOUNG MAN: That's enough! You think I'll tell anyone? Would you expect that?

YOUNGEST SISTER: I wouldn't.

YOUNG MAN: What more do you want? Haven't we been to the movies many times? Your mother knows it, too. What did I do?

YOUNGEST SISTER: That's different.

YOUNG MAN: I even dodged the other girl, because of you.
I said, Father, I will not marry this girl. Told him I had someone to
marry already. We were promised, I said.
YOUNGEST SISTER: (*Delighted*) Did you really say that?
YOUNG MAN: Of course I did. Are you kidding? Just wait,
I'll take you to my father and say, here, this is the one! Huh? What
do you say? Okay?
NARRATOR: The boy did what the giantess told. He took
the Three Oranges, got down without even looking back…

(*The button is pushed; the sound is cut off.*)

DIRECTOR: Well… where was the boy?
PRODUCER: At a bar.
DIRECTOR: No, not that one, the one in the tale?
PRODUCER: In the garden, he has the oranges and now he's
taking them… The youngest sister is somewhat weak. Bright lights, a
little glitter and she's blown away.
DIRECTOR: There's alcohol, too; of course the system of
values will collapse. The girl has no moral values whatsoever anyway.
Her mother made it easy, too.

(*The button is pushed, the tape resumes.*)

[…]

Translated by Arzu Akbatur and Nilgün Dungan

'Üç Turunçlar' Necatigil, Behçet. *Radyo Oyunları*. Istanbul: Yapı Kredi Yayınları, 2009.

'*I*', an Essay

I

Yet I was just about to do such and such, what a marvelous excuse you are: It is because of you that I…

Every *I* is a narration of a bickering about a *you*, in a roundabout manner since my place is somewhere between *you* and him and it is not *he* who is close to my heart but you. If *I* were me I would classify the singular pronouns in grammar books in the following order: *you, I, he! You* comes first as there is no such thing as *I* if there is no *you*. Every *I* becomes conscious of itself through *you*. So what if it does? It then attempts to rage against, to resist this self, and in the end fails as it is only *you* that cares for him. *I*, as precious as it might deem itself to be, alone is nothing but hot air!

By itself *I* does not exist, but nor does *you*. Should they have a run-in, now that could get ugly. It's a different story for *he* and *I*, their affair is a bit more harmless as *he* is always more removed and one may take any number of precautions as long as there is that distance in between.

There is something unnerving about *you*, this much is clear from Özdemir Asaf, who didn't say just *you* but instead, *You You You*, as if raging, bitter lament, *Oh You!*

Just imagine, the use of *if* in both the subjunctive and the conditional mood. So even if *I* wishes for something, that wish is tied up to a condition: it is only if *you* obliges! So what does this prove, you ask? That *I* is merely a beginning. The middle and the end are shaped, set on a path, or reversely led astray and exhausted at the hand of *you*. Fuzûlî posed the question '*Ger ben ben isem nesin sen ey yar,*' which meant: 'How am I to remain as myself as long as you exist, as long as there is you!' Every second person is one that changes me. And what of yet another, a third? A savior to return me to myself perhaps! Yet every *he* that comes too close will become *you*, and so the same drama all over again.

'You and I don't exist, only we do' is true only in the land of the Epic. In the Lyric world it would be right to say we do not exist, but you do. The whole poem is formed around you: ballads, elegies about love, separation and pain, all because of a *you*.

The *-de* suffix of a noun in Turkish signals a sense of groundedness and tranquility. Not as if en route somewhere but rather being there. In exactly the same way, I wish I too were with/in/*I*. (Half the reason why I love *Divan* poetry is because of its generous use of puns). So as not to be with/out/*you*, I wish I were with/in/*I*. And when I am with/in/*I*, you can take a deep breath, because I have stayed my ground, because I am now your slave.

This *I* always reminds me of the [Turkish] word *bugün*, for 'today'. When written separately (*bu gün*) *bu* serves as an adjective qualifying 'day', literally meaning 'this day'; but when joined, the single word acts as an adverb of time with the meaning of now, on this very day. We should have been able to use such word combinations as *thisI* (*buben*), so as to convey the meaning of *I* better, so as to reveal its meaning connected to time, since there is always the notion of now, present time, hidden within the *I*. How could the *I* of yesterday be the same as the *I* of today? This *I* is a sum of all *thisI*'s: as Asaf Halet Çelebi[1] said, 'With every step I take / I place infinite *I*'s / into the emptiness'. Yet there is something odd about its relationship with *you*. While *this I*'s are as tightly bound up with you as they are by time, just like 'today', *this I* seems to have escaped, has almost become free of you. Doesn't this duality then prove the states of freedom and captivity of the *I* attached to *you* and the *I* that is separate from *you*?

If I were to prepare an interview, these would be the questions I'd pose: why is it that the suppressed anxiety in almost all the answers an artist gives when being questioned betrays a kind of 'an averting of oneself altogether' 'a self-defense'? Or why is it that artists them selves are unable to see certain contradictions so easily caught on by others when they write or speak of their own work?

---

1 Asaf Halet Çelebi (1907-1958) '*her adımımda/sonsuzben'lerikoyuyorum/ boşluğa...*' from his poem 'Adımlar'.

Why is it that there is a sense of emptiness, collapse, nothingness, or futility that takes hold of us at the end of love affairs, the first weeks of school holidays in empty classrooms, when we come across the printed versions of our articles or books approved for publication, when we hear from the mouths of others things we believe to be true ourselves?

Why is it that when we are praised or picked apart by others or when we reveal to them ourselves, unmasked, why is it that our cheeks burn red hot as if we have committed the greatest of crimes? Why…
Even questions of this kind show that there is an *I* that exists in us, unchanged in spite of everything, that in spite of all the *you*'s, we have remained *I* – because these humdrum questions are posed in the absence of *you*. And it feels good to be able to say I am me!

Translated by Alev Ersan

'Ben' from Necatigil, Behçet. *Bile/Yazdı.*Yapı Kredi Yayınları 2015.
(first published by Ada Yayınları in 1979) 'Şiir Burçları' from Necatigil, Behçet. *Bile/Yazdı.*Yapı Kredi Yayınları 2015.(first published by Ada Yayinlari in 1979)

[**Every thing is a translation**]

Every thing is a translation
Different is the translation of the same thing
Examples:
Whether his eyes were open or shut he could see it
Eyes open or shut
With eyes, he could se-
His eyes….. he could see it
In between a change, such as this:
Let's say he could see it
With what could he see? Let's say with his eyes.

Every thing is a translation
We turn everything (in)to/wards ourselves
According to the self every thing
Changes   fragments
Let's say 'He kept seeing it' is what we mean
This we may render in different ways
Examples:
Whether his eyes were open or shut…
Eyes open or shut…
Even if his eyes were shut…
He opens his eyes, he shuts them, and yet…
His eyes……
He kept seeing it (and so on)
In between, forms change
Depending on our taste,
Turn the armchair this way or that
It's the same old chair
But
Still
Some things have changed!

I turn everything (in)to/wards myself
There's difference in the details
How we view a news flash, an anguish or an expression of love
Is one thing to your mind's eye, quite another to mine.

Translated by Saliha Paker,
with the 10th Cunda International Workshop for Translators of
Turkish Literature

[Her şey bir çeviri] from Necatigil, Behçet. *Şiirler: Bütün Yapıtları*. Istanbul: Yapı
Kredi Yayınları, 2014.

Horoscope

Which water the water of life
So your fortune shows
You are on the cusp of exile.

A time just slipping by
A train or perhaps a ship
You too are on board it.

On emerging into dark
None emerge who know
You are in the house of wisdom.

Translated by Neil P. Doherty

'Burç,' from *Kareler Aklar*. Necatigil, Behçet. *Şiirler: Bütün Yapıtları*, Istanbul: Yapı Kredi Yayınları, 2014.(*Varlık, 804,* September 1974)

The Houses of Horoscope in Poetry

Which house are you ruled by? This one or that! I can't say I much believe in readers of horoscope who upon studying charts of constellations either foretell people of their prospects or warn against an impending doom, yet I take houses of horoscope in poetry to be much different than mere probability, but rather as pointers of such truths that vary little.

I believe that every poet in the course of his life moves through three houses of horoscope: the house of Exile, the house of Longing and the house of Wisdom. In the course of the first house, the poet experiences exile for a while. Like Robinson, he has been cast away on a desert island. He builds a shelter with whatever he can lay his hands on. A self-preservation instinct of some kind urges him to build a hut, a roof, some proof of his existence. He is not entirely conscious of what he writes and the part coincidence plays is great during this time. His appreciation for literature is not really set on solid ground. It might be good poets or bad poets that he admires. He is fortunate if he has run into some of the great names of his day. He will write just like them, exactly the same perhaps, or maybe better. Nevertheless he is a copycat, the work produced in these years is an imitation, a search for oneself. He may be found to amount to nothing more than an echo of a poet of his own time. This is the house of Exile. How much time one remains here depends on the poet himself.

Next, he enters the second house, that of Longing. The poet longs for his own poetry and realizes that it is a waste of time to hang about in the house of Exile. He can now see how much of himself there is in his own work and how much there is of others. He is filled with a longing for himself. This yearning reaches a point of saturation, becomes clear. Now all his protests, his anxiety, take a singular, a personal shape. He discovers his own perspective, his mode of writing in this period. His obsessions, his beliefs deepen vertically. The rings on the water's surface have now become concentric circles, they crash into the shore with greater force. The poet, as if enraptured, follows his own trail, on a quest that reaches further into himself; it is in this time of longing that he reveals himself, his own world, with unruly vigor.
Time passes. Then all of a sudden it dawns on him. He realizes the

difficulty of shaping one's environment, the world, to one's will. Happiness (let's say that of a certain environment with particular boundaries or an immensity, say the happiness of the world) has still not been attained. He understands this. He understands that he has not been able to quench even his own modest desires; he has not inspired any change in his immediate environment. Out of all that he has manifested, all that he has revived, what portion of it has been taken in, to what degree has his word been heard? What was it all for? Why ever did he write it all? All of this dawns on him.

And thereon he enters the house of Wisdom. Wisdom is complex and it changes little. It is here that he truly understands the great poets of the past. Why each and everyone of them for a time wrote from a place of despair, how they become akin to Yunus*, to Khayyam, to Galip* with the recognition that time outside of us eats away ever so quickly at the time within. The poet enters, more than anything else, the period of his unchanging destiny. Fate, which is not the same as destiny, has a place even in the most developed of civilizations. He has tired of it all. He has yearned for it, yet it has not come about and he is now wearied. Where does one take refuge now? He passes through to the house of Wisdom. The poems of protest, of revolution, are replaced by the poetry of acceptance, consent, and the poetry of letting go.

Look up wisdom in a dictionary, you'll find: experience, a mysterious cause, God's great plan, undecipherable to us humans. And for all great poets there has come a time, whether it's before their day or not, that they have come under the rule of this house. And what remains in the end is mostly I believe the poetry of the house of Wisdom. It is the house of Wisdom that reveals the immovable fortune of man because exile is temporary, and so is longing and the eternal man prevails in the house of wisdom.

Ali Şîr Nevaî* collected the poetry of different periods of his life into four separate volumes, childhood, youth, middle age, old age, embellishing the titles with terms in turn as 'Wonders, Rarities, Marvels, Benefits'. If we take childhood and youth to be the same period, then it comes to the same notion as the three houses of horoscope: people first write 'estranged poems in exile' then 'beautiful poems in longing' and poems that account for a lifetime are those 'we benefit from in our wisdom'.

We speak of houses of horoscope, a phrase borrowed from astrology, but what of forts, houses of fortification? Structures with ridges jutting out. Rounded, rectangular or hexagonal battlements of fortresses? We might dwell on these structures of poetry too. The poet Nâbî*, at the end of his well-known *gazel* with the refrain 'nothing remains' says, 'Where should the supplicants (*niyaz ehli*) take refuge from the assault of the armies of gloom (*gam askerleri*)? No battlement, no rampart remains from the fortress of Endeavor, nothing remains'. The Poet too is a *niyaz ehli*, someone hoping, waiting ,wishing; fighting the armies of gloom, in other words, despair, which are all the troubles that vex and worry him. The poet, how will he fend for himself against time that erodes all, gnawing at everything?

As forts of poetry come crashing down one after the other, it is only true poetry that remains, whichever house of horoscope it may be ruled by; it withstands the force of time like unshakable fortresses, till the end of time. True poetry does not easily become a toothless grin in the ruins of a bastion.

And yet most poets are satisfied with remaining in the house of Exile and the house of Longing. They exert their powers through these domains. It is as though they have found what they had been looking for and were not in need of anything more. Yet the eyes of the mature reader will seek the poetry of the final house, the house of Wisdom, since man, perhaps not in the beginning but in the end, will be inescapably alone. What is it that remains at the end, this is what needs to be determined. Is it exile, longing, or wisdom? When we look at the Islamic classics of the East, their exile and longing seem pretentious to us. Yet if those exiles and longings are bound to wisdom, then they keep flashing on and off like lighthouses in the dark. Within the mortar of the fortresses they've built is a filling of wisdom, not grit. And with wisdom they have all remained.

Translated by Alev Ersan

* Yunus Emre, 13thC Anatolian mystic poet; Galip (1751799) Ottoman Divan poet and Mevlevi Sheik; Ali Şîr Nevaî (1441-1501) Chagatay (Eastern Turkic) poet; Nâbî (1642-1712) Ottoman Divan poet

A Selection of Works by Other Poets

Ahmet Haşim (1884 - 1933)

Ahmet Haşim was born in Baghdad in 1884 to an old Ottoman family. In 1896, he was sent to Istanbul to learn Turkish and receive an Ottoman education. He became interested in French and Ottoman poetry at the Sultanî (Galatasaray) High School and published his first poem in 1901. After graduating in 1907, he held various low-level bureaucratic and teaching posts. During World War I, he was a reserve officer and inspector in the Ottoman Army. After discharge, he again had to accept various low-level posts. His first poetry collection, *Göl Saatleri*, was published in 1921 and his second collection, *Piyale*, in 1928. He travelled to Paris and Frankfurt a few times, mostly for medical care. He was engaged various times but never married. He died in Istanbul in 1933. His poetry was influential in integrating French symbolism into Ottoman poetic forms.

Birds in Black

Birds settling on crimson reeds and ruby water,
souls that feed on blood and setting suns,
in silence and sorrow feed till filled
on sun, bloody bodiless head on the horizon.

Translated by Donny Smith

'Siyah Kuşlar' from *Göl Saatleri*, 1921. *Servet-i Fünûn*, 1911.

Storks in the Moonlight

Poisêd in a line on the water's edge they wait,
dreamy storks, to dive into the moon's spell.
The heavens tonight reflect a lake, in the air,
as though suddenly insects had become stars...
But why are there no fish or frogs in these celestial waters?
What bird could eat these swarming tiny creatures of light?
Souls and eyes are in waiting on this mystery, as though
dreamy storks, to dive into the moon's spell.

Translated by Donny Smith

'Mehtâbta Leylekler' from *Göl Saatleri*, 1921. Servet-i Fünûn, 1911.

Bats

Like scattered autumnal veils
These nightbirds noiselessly flutter.
They come, they go...as though braiding
Stars of grief with dark of night.

Translated by Donny Smith

'Yarasalar' from *Göl Saatleri*, 1921. Rübab, 1913.

Stair

With slow step after step you climb these stairs
with your skirts heaped with sun-colored leaves,
and for a time, you look at the heavens and weep …

The waters have gone yellow, and bit by bit your face has gone pale.
Keep watch in the crimson sky, for something is coming …

Bent toward the soil, the roses bleed and bleed,
with bloody nightingales waiting on branches like flames.
Have the waters caught fire? Why is the marble red like bronze?

This is a secret language that fills the soul.
Keep watch in the crimson sky, for evening is coming …

Translated by Donny Smith

Merdiven

Ağır ağır çıkacaksın bu merdivenlerden,
Eteklerinde güneş rengi bir yığın yaprak,
Ve bir zaman bakacaksın semâya ağlayarak...

Sular sarardı... yüzün perde perde solmakta
Kızıl hevâları seyret ki bir şey olmakta...

Eğilmiş arza, kanar, muttasıl kanar güller;
Durur alev gibi dallarda kanlı bülbüller,
Sular mı yandı? Neden tunca benziyor mermer?

Bu bir lisan-ı hafîdir ki rûha dolmakta,
Kızıl hevâları seyret ki akşam olmakta.

Temmuz 336

'Merdiven' from *Piyale*, 1926. Şebab, 1920.

Forest

What flows is not water but the season's changing,
the sound in your ear of leaf and branch.
What clashes in the darkness is the stars' twinkling
against the water, again and again.

Translated by Donny Smith

'Satırlar' from *Piyale*, 1926. Yeni Mecmua, 1923.

Nazım Hikmet (1902 – 1963)

Nazım Hikmet, who is Turkey's most internationally renowned poet, was born in 1902 in Salonica (present-day Thessaloniki). During the 1920s, he studied Economics and Sociology in Moscow, where he was influenced by Russian art and political views. An outspoken communist, he was imprisoned during the 1940s for his political views and an international campaign was organized for his release. His poetry blends the personal with the political, all the while retaining a lyrical style, and in addition to poetry he wrote plays and memoirs. He spent much of his later life in exile in Russia, and died there in 1963.

A City

I climbed several hills I turned a few corners and walked
I walked and walked I followed my nose
                    a door opened I entered
                            I lost myself in myself

a city I didn't know
houses of shapes I'd never seen
some swarming with people some completely empty
some a window from floor to ceiling some a blank wall
I veered into a street muddy narrow crooked
it brought me around to an old part
I came out to an asphalt thoroughfare the central avenue
it stretched away to the dawn straight and wide
in one quarter it rains
                    next door there is sun
                            in the third moonlight

I crossed a bridge
lights gleamed halfway
                    half was pitchblack
I saw two trees side by side
on one not a leaf stirs
the other moans and roars writhing in pain
nothing resembles anything else in a city
                    apart from the people
all of them twins or triplets or quintuplets in tens and millions
all cowards
          all heroes
          all fools
               all wise
                    all swine
                         all angels.

Translated by Ruth Christie

'Bir Şehir' from *Son Şiirleri*, September 7, 1961 Leipzig.

Bir Şehir

Bir kaç yokuş tırmandım bir iki dönemeç döndüm ve yürüdüm
burnumun doğrusuna yürüdüm yürüdüm
                bir kapı açıldı girdim
                yitirdim kendimi kendi içimde

bilmediğim bir şehir
görmediğim biçimde evleri
kimi karınca yuvası kimi bomboş
kimi baştan aşağı pencere kimi kör duvar
bir sokağa saptım çamurlu dar eğri büğrü
dönüp dolaştırdı getirdi beni eski yere
asfalt bir caddeyi çıktım bulvar ortası
uzayıp gidiyor tan yerine kadar dosdoğru geniş
bir mahallede yağmur yağıyor
                  bitişiğinde güneş
                  üçüncüsünde ayışığı
bir köprü geçtim
yarısında fenerler pırıl pırıl
                  yarısı kapkaranlıktı
yan yana iki ağaç gördüm
yaprak kımıldamıyor birinde
öbürü kıvrana kıvrana inleyip haykırıyor
bir şehirde bir birine benzemiyor hiçbir şey
                  insanları bir yana
onların hepsi ikizdi üçüzdü beşizdi onuzdu milyonuzdu
hepsi korkak
  hepsi yiğit
    hepsi aptal
      hepsi akıllıydı
        hepsi domuzdu
          hepsi melekti

Melih Cevdet Anday (1915 - 2002)

Melih Cevdet Anday's long career stretched from the nineteen-forties into the twenty-first century. In 1941, he and his friends Oktay Rifat and Orhan Veli published *Garip* ('Strange'), a little book of poems that severed the new Turkish poetic tradition decisively from its Ottoman past and set the terms for modern Turkish verse. Sidney Wade and Efe Murad have just recently completed translating this book.

Sparrow

My little sparrow,
Sitting on a clothesline hung with laundry!
Are you looking at me with pity?
In any case, I'm keeping my eye on you
As you fly under the sun
And the first white leaves.

Translated by Sidney Wade and Efe Murad

'Serçe' from *Garip*, Istanbul: Resimli Ay Matbaası, 1941.

All Over Again

I was sick in bed for three whole months.
Didn't know who I was,
Or the city streets.
I forgot how to play backgammon
And the face of my beloved.
How beautiful it is now to begin
Walking and loving, all over again!

Translated by Sidney Wade and Efe Murad

'Yeni Baştan' from *Garip*, Istanbul: Resimli Ay Matbaası, 1941.
Yeni Baştan (*Varlık, no. 185*)

Second World War

How could I have waited until today
To not speak of death?
Is it possible I didn't recognize it?
At work my cigarette is bitter.
It's no longer possible to fall in love.
Waking up has lost its charm.
I was born during the First World War,
Why did we need a second one?
Just so I could pay my dues?

Translated by Sidney Wade and Efe Murad

'İkinci Harbi Umumi' from *Garip*, Istanbul: Resimli Ay Matbaası 1941.

To Whistle

To the fish, an ocean is necessary.
To make love, you must be unemployed.
And in bed at night,
To feel no pain in the soles of your feet,
You must be rich.
But in order to whistle,
You need nothing at all.

Translated by Sidney Wade and Efe Murad

'Islık Çalmak' from *Garip*, Istanbul: Resimli Ay Matbaası 1941.

Cemal Süreya (1931 - 1990)

Cemal Süreya was born in eastern Turkey in 1931 to an Alevi Zaza (Kurdish) family. After the Dersim Rebellion, his family was sent into internal exile in western Turkey. Eventually Cemal Süreya graduated from the prestigious Haydarpaşa High School in Istanbul and then from Ankara University, after which he held various posts in the Turkish government. His first collection, *Üvercinka*, won the 1959 Yeditepe Poetry Prize and is often considered the first book of the Second New poetry movement, a reaction to and synthesis of previous movements in Turkish poetry, with strong influence from French surrealism. He published the influential literary magazine *Papirüs* intermittently from 1960 to 1981. His poetry collection *Göçebe* won the 1966 Turkish Language Association Poetry Prize, and his collections *Sıcak Nal* and *Güz Bitiği* won the 1988 Behçet Necatigil Poetry Prize. He was married various times and had two children. He died in Istanbul in 1990.

Middle East IV

Time? No, not time.
What flows is not time but distance.
The sun's hammer above
The water's knife below
The chromium modest, the copper shy,
The tree: a single drop of water between two sparks.
The wind knows not whence it will blow,
The borders have been cut,
Flashes of light in the settlements.
We have been broken, we will be broken even more
But the killer does not know whom he will kill
Nor does the thief know what he will steal
We are novices in a new life
Everything we know is being reshaped
Our poetry, our love
Perhaps we are living the end of our evil days

Or perhaps we will live the beginning of our good days
Something astringent is in the air
Between past and future
Between pain and joy
Between anger and forgiveness.
We have been broken, we will be broken even more
From East to West, in all the world
But the dagger with which brother strikes brother
Forges a bond between two hearts
It will grow - one day - and there it will become richer,
For the elixir that will resurrect Ali
Is hidden in the poison that is given to Hasan
And this granite, its aliveness will become an ocean,
The rivers will flow with more docility,
As a flower opens on its own
As a bird flies
Thus human beings will love and will work
The barrenness that strikes the mountains
Makes the rose migrate through the dawn
Through nature's golden dawn
Through humanity's golden dawn
Through history's golden dawn.
And we have been broken, and we will be broken even more

But no one can touch our innocence.

Translated by Donny Smith

'Ortadoğu IV' from *Beni Öp Sonra Doğur Beni*, 1973. *Papirüs*, 1966.
Sevda Sözleri: Bütün Şiirleri. 25 ed. İstanbul: Yapı Kredi Yayınları, 2005.

Cevat Çapan (1933 -)

Cevat Çapan is a poet, translator, and a lecturer in English Literature. He was born in Kocaeli in 1933 and studied at the University of Cambridge. He has worked for the BBC as well as the Department of English Language and Literature at Istanbul University, where he became a professor in 1975. His first published poem appeared in the Turkish literary magazine *Varlik* in 1952, and since then he has published many books of poetry and translation.

Crete

In the evenings
we'd sit and talk by the doorway
with the old women waiting.

Their questioning eyes would ask,
shall we ever return,
wrenched from our homes, displaced,
to the lands
where we feel our roots running deep?

This wind that blows
would carry salt
from the pebbly shores
of an island distanced
in time's sea.

When they opened the bridal-chests
to air the garments
the orange colour would fade,
and mosquito nets
sway on the balcony
in the damp sea-mist…

On the horizon a ship would appear
and vanish.

Translated by Ruth Christie

'Crete' from *Su Sesi*. Istanbul: Yapı Kredi Yayınları, 2013.

A Retired Chief Engineer

So you were picking wild strawberries before you went home,
before the cyanide could mingle with the springs,
this year your trees gave so many chestnuts.
And don't forget the lüfer season just beginning
         on the Bosphorus.

I know you don't keep track of everything,
of whether you put the clocks right or not.
Your aunt Kiraz has sent you a skin of curd cheese from the village,
and an earthenware jar of honeycomb for the children.
When winter comes, you'll tell them lengthy tales
         of the Partridge Well,
of Ağagil's golden mare, his Circassian saddle you leapt on
and how you softened your leather sandals
dried up from the heat,
         in the stream's cool waters.

I thought we might set out early one morning
to look for the famous serpent on Alemdağ.
If it carried us off to Scheherazade,
Scheherazade could fly us to the stories with no end
         in the Phoenix's arbour.

Translated by Ruth Christie

'Emekli Baş Mühendis' from *Su Sesi*. Istanbul: Yapı Kredi Yayınları, 2013.

Yalıoba Diary IV

Heading south over the mountains, the closer to shore
        the more dry riverbeds you'll see.
Once on Ida's many-crested slopes were pinetrees
        uniting earth and sky,
and fertile orchards, kitchen gardens flourishing on the plain.
Today on the foothills of Ida - the poet called her
mother of wild beasts and many streams -
you'll meet instead a horde of crazy drivers hurtling from the scene.
        *

Now we're at a wedding in the old mill above the Mıhlı Stream
        that falls to the wide-armed gulf.
Pursuing happiness, the bridegroom dives into cold waters that pour
        under lofty planetrees,
while the bride surveys the sea of islands and adjusts her veil.
        *

Now other barbarians despoil the lands once famous for Achilles
who boasted he'd delete the lot without a trace.
        Long ago
in the well-watered valleys were heard the laments
        of women weeping in pain.
Now we hear wonder echoing in the waters
        for Assos' sunken harbour with its marble columns.
        *

Night and silence. Those who remained imagined
        that somehow the departed would soon return,
but the long watching lasted days and nights.
Some days they amused themselves for a while with letters,
        the letters came to nothing.
The watchers' hair grew white, the departed never came back,
        in time forgotten.

Translated by Ruth Christie

'Yalıoba Günlüğü' from *Su Sesi*. Istanbul: Yapı Kredi Yayınları, 2013.

The Voice of Water

Their names were first inscribed in the Book of Snow,
as the snows melted in spring
          they disappeared -
but imprinted in nature's memory, those names
reappeared in the warmth of spring.
Some in flowers dewy with morning,
some in evening's glow on the horizon.

*

The end of June
summer had begun with the north-east wind,
with no let-up for weeks
waves beat on the rocks.
On Tenedos Homer's voice
          mixed with the sound of wind
and the screams of seagulls.

*

And near the end of July -
in the wind's invisible cradle
          poplar leaves tremble,
the waters of the swollen river churn in the bay
          alive with power even

Translated by Ruth Christie

'Su Sesi' from *Su Sesi*. Istanbul: Yapı Kredi Yayınları, 2013.

Gülten Akın (1933 - 2015)

Gülten Akın was born in Yozgat in 1933. She studied law at Ankara University and worked as a lawyer and teacher for many years in various parts of Anatolia where she traveled with her husband and children. One of the pioneers of 20th century Turkish literature, her early poems were more informed by personal ideas and experiences, while her more mature work focused on social issues. In her poetry she strived for simplicity and a desire to be understood by the ordinary reader. She won many awards for her work, and her final book of poems, *Beni Sorarsan*, was published in 2013.

Composed

I am like a book of poetry
out of prison
as I have been re-written
I am getting heavier, quieter
in old idiom more composed
marked and underlined here and there

Translated by Yusuf Eradam

One Line

Word assails, hush flees.

Translated by Yusuf Eradam

'Asude' from *Beni Sorarsan*, Istanbul: Yapı Kredi Yayınları, 2013, 2016.
'Tek Dize' from *Beni Sorarsan*, Istanbul: Yapı Kredi Yayınları, 2013, 2016.

Ahmet Ada (1947 - 2016)

Ahmet Ada was born in Ceyhan in the province of Adana in 1947. He worked in various cities throughout Turkey as a civil servant, retiring in 1993 to devote himself to poetry. His first volume of poetry was published in 1980, and he went on to publish another 24 volumes before his untimely death in March 2016. His poetry is marked by an extraordinary lyricism and a willingness to experiment with longer epic-like sequences and more unusual forms. In addition, he wrote a number of works of criticism and a book of poetics.

Looking

for Cavafy

In the market at Mersin
for a house set in a garden
of my chidhood, for
wounds. For the hours
beside that house set in a garden.
in Mersin I wander
Find, if you can,
youth. A smell
there at the Mersin Hotel
In the night street, just beyond me
The scent of roses
that follow me everywhere.
is a a corner
where watermelons

I am looking
for the lost language
the scab of its
I spent kicking ball in the lot
Now through the marketplace
books under my arm.
wherever it was you set down your
a dazzling smell within me
where I am staying.
an army of lilies.
the enchanted oleander
Yet all I am looking for
lit by a smoky lamp
are sold.

Translated by Neil P. Doherty

Arayış

Kavafis'e

Mersin çarşında   bahçeli evi
ararım.   Çocukluğumun yitik
dilini, kabuk   bağlayan
yaralarını. Bahçeli evin   yanındaki
arsada akşama dek   top
koşturduğum saatleri.   Şimdi sürtüyorum
koltuğumda kitaplar   Mersin çarşısında.
Ara ki bulasın   koyduğun yerde
gençliğini. Bir koku   içim baş döndüren bir koku
Mersin Oteli'nde   yatar kalkarım.
Gece, sokakta, az ötemde   zambakgillerden bir ordu.
Ve gül kokusu,   tılsımlı zakkum
peşimi bırakmıyor   Oysa ben isli bir lamba
ışığında   karpuz satılan
bir köşe başı   ararım.

'Arayış' from *Sonsuz At-Seçme Şiirleri*. Şiirden Yayıncılık, 2009.

From the sequence 'Love'

Love I

through my soul runs a blue mare
a soaring happiness

through the plain runs a blue fox
her breath the cold of february
into the woods turns her sly shade
skipping from stone to stone

happiness even this pain in my heart
like imagining a young girl
and her burnt cherry lips
right in the middle of a lovely day

and still the blue mare runs
through my maddened soul

Translated by Neil P. Doherty

'Aşk I' from *Taşın Sesi*. Şiirden Yayıncılık, 2014.

Love II

i found the happiness i'd lost
in the gallop of a white sea bound horse
the haze of dawn was soaring
yesterday in the horse's packsaddle.

by the rose i fell defeated
then scattered but love i found
on touching the pure, the clear silk
my joy soared in the scent of its skin.

in the gallop of a white sea bound horse
i was left all out of breath
my fair joy crumbling to grain
i became a river returning to the sea.

i found her mouth all strawberry scented
yesterday her mouth filled my mouth
shame crumbled to grain on her face
my breath became, a white horse

Translated by Neil P. Doherty

'Aşk II' from *Taşın Sesi*. Şiirden Yayıncılık, 2014.

Love III

the night's red comes not from the sky
but from your hair, from thick veined leaves
what is forgotten: stone, sand and pebble
under our feet there on the shore
a tree, mute nature embracing you

love i say this receding stone
this approaching land, this reddening night
your hours become the world
the forest i plunged into

love i say this love in me
poverty of the plain, plenty of the forest,
when glanced from here
an internal bleeding of ten years

red the ringing silence of the night
i part the flower of the dark
making the most unpardonable mistakes

Translated by Neil P. Doherty

'Aşk III' from *Taşın Sesi*. Şiirden Yayıncılık, 2014.

Love IV

one day a person understands
the worth of a face washed
in snowflakes, the softest of hair
and a row of poplars surrounding the house

ah from my veins flow the stirring
of the world, the noise of the birds
streets, streets ah the streets
they remember your face washed
in snowflakes

how strongly i had grown attached
to the light of the whirling snow, of eyes
glowing like snow that assuage fear
that stir the sand and the pebble
awake

ah but my boat is sinking
& the lake is receding from the house
you are no longer by my side
my boat is tattered and torn

Translated by Neil P. Doherty

'Aşk IV' from *Taşın Sesi*. Şiirden Yayıncılık, 2014.

Lâle Müldür (1956 -)

Lâle Müldür was born in 1956 in Aydın, Turkey. More than 10 collections of her poetry have been published, and she wrote the novel *Bizansiyya*. Two collections of her poetry, *Water Music* and *I too Went to the Hunt of the Deer*, are available in English translation, and a collection of her work has been translated into French: *Ainsi parle la fille de pluie* / Yağmur Kızı Böyle Diyor. Some of her poems have been set to music, most famously '*Destina*,' by the band Yeni Türkü. She is currently living in Istanbul.

A Red Indian Summer

I

the shore's one side is water
the other cinnamon
lost knowledge
craves to return
the sun pales on its ice island
I never saw you in my dreams
look, around us everything is crying
my face hangs out of the window
I should have said, 'no! no!'
I wiped out your name and wrote a poem
desperate for distance
when you hold me close
I will let myself go
fearing the dark's eyes, fearing
and for each passing summer the Indians
will put a horse chestnut to one side
and all this week it will rain
and all this week I won't think of you
but I'll think of the trace of our star in the sky
and later a woman will leave me
in the heart of melancholy
as rain flows from huts, gutters, forests
a woman wrapped in the rain
Soledad
will bring me a deep, dark leaf
in a glacial sunrise
that jaguarial, river of jaguars
Uranus' moons are weeping
on the dark shore seen in dreams

II

that which passed between us
like infinite water
for a summer
a summer
defined by knives
of Indians and tigers
there is a lonely moment
as long as a vein
that statues ressurected
between you and revenge
no, don't remember anything
apart from an endless summer
and yet how many times more
will they bleed, our eyes
like red seaweeds
who knows how many times more
in other endless summers
the refractive wave
was the rupture place
this is why I say
it was just an endless summer
remember nothing else

Translated by Caroline Stockford

'Kızılderili bir Yaz' from *Anemon*. Istanbul: Yapı Kredi Yayıncılık, 4th imprint, 2014.

Tierra del Fuego

Between sea shells, among seaweed.
Those dark objects of the underwater world.
Is your image.
In the Siamese cats I see in my dreams.

ON THE WALLS OF ODARA.

In the cracks in ODARA walls.
In the place where distinctive claw marks you left
on me begin and end. YOUR FACE IS THERE.

.

That hut where we slept to the song
of the 'Poinciana' tree and sound of waves.
On those stretching sands where our shadows
mixed together. Those diamond points that light disintegrates forever.

POINTS OF ANNIHILATION. Your eyes. Violet purple

or cyclamen you said.
Sing 'Canta Mais' one more time...

.

A GREY PUMA had hidden behind a tree.
You used to hide your heart like a black animal.
Poisonous as an anaconda and lonely
as a solitarius, you were. The moment, one day
when I saw me in the mirror and not another
'everything will end' you said.

.

I WAS BESIDE A CLOUDY STRETCH OF WATER

as you set off for Estrada do Sol.
I could hear your voice despite all that distance.
Then, then, I lost your voice, the shapes your face would take.
Mine reminding me of things trifling, trivial.
For example, that day I glimpsed you from behind.
A sentence you left unfinished. 'The river the Pampero
passengers were forced to cross..'

.

Then, why, whenever I have to remember you
do foolish things come to my mind?
My telling you of long, long jaguars,
mangoes, grapes from India.
How stunned I was, later, to learn that
FISH sleep with eyes open.

.

Your thinking: 'How easy it is to influence this girl
with silly, senseless things'. Or maybe,
my thinking you thought that.
My thinking you thought that is once again

my thinking's projection.
Thoughts of my thoughts... memories of my memories…

.

Those days I always wanted to go to Tierra del Fuego. In the pickup
Gato Barbieri, Carlos Jobim, Baden Powell were constantly on 'Play'.
Antonio, Yo le Canto a la Luna, Falando de Amor, Saudades de Bahia...
The Girl from Ipanema, Bolivia... For days, without leaving my room
I would think of the tropics.
Tropicus... Mar del Tropicus...
They thought I thought of the Tropics – they misunderstood.
Or was this a reaction to sleepy, sterile cultures.
Longing for a primitive sound.

The search, once more, for the mystery.
Maybe it was an escape. A far, far escape.
If only they knew all the things I want to escape.

.

'WE'LL NEVER COMPREHEND THE MAYA'

Something really is happening here. A mystical thing.
As sublime and strange as the underwater world.
Watching the rain from the window on a grey day.
Lucid dragonflies slowly pull away, bringing me
to you in topaz temples.
You smile just like a sun god.
Do you know how many years I'm on my own,
in confusion.
You see, I just couldn't loosen my grip.
I walked by your side, yours alone
on a topaz day by the waterside.
At night you would pull a cover over me.
We wouldn't speak for considerable time.
I'd lose myself in your eyes.

This state of not speaking was a perceptible thing.
Like the silence of a river running
through sea and darkness.

.

Do you know, something's happening here. A strange thing.
Like annihilation in cloudy water
White butterflies are flying in my eyes
and they're bringing me to myself slowly,
in rooms of white...

.

My forgetting was a different you. I was dying Tropico.
Dying with the white romance of your forgetting.

I have nothing left to say anymore.
But then neither did I want to forget.
Because there are wounds that stay beautiful, too.
There are lemon scented, rainy women...
Women you'll never forget...lemon scented...
despite it all...there are women that stay as rain...

*

I'm fine now. How are you?

Translated by: Caroline Stockford

'Tierra del Fuego' from *Anemon*. Istanbul: Yapı Kredi Yayıncılık, 4th imprint, 2014.

Sami Baydar (1962 - 2012)

Sami Baydar was born in 1962 in Merzifon. He studied painting in the Istanbul Academy of Fine Arts from 1979-87. During this period he began publishing poems in a literary magazine called *Beyaz*, and his first book, *Dünya Efendiler*, was published in the same year as he graduated from the Istanbul Academy. He published six more collections of poetry, including his collected poems, *Dünya İnancı*, which was published in 2012, a mere month after his untimely death. Throughout his writing life Sami Baydar, in the words of Haydar Ergülen, 'wrote poetry in order to make sense of the world, indeed to give meaning to the world'. In doing so he left behind a startling body of poetry that seems to stand outside any poetic school or movement. He also left behind two collections of short stories and a large body of visual work in his paintings. Indeed Sami Bayder had just begun to exhibit his work internationally before he died on the October 29, 2012.

Desert

What's your name
what's yours
I asked first
there are no princes here
nothing of interest here
galaxies, stars
it was you I loved the most
what do you say to speaking of the sky
or of sand storms
they blind people
storms of the desert
that do not stop till they've covered everything
bring me good luck
we have accomplished something difficult
like a sand lizard
we stepped out into the world
clean & beautiful
in the desert water is more precious than gold
really water is so lovely
I'd always water the flowers
& you, you are giving water to a poor stranger
that is the end of everything
sand, everywhere sand
no water to be found in the desert
a scorching desert sun
I will surely have gone mad from thirst
just there by the palm trees
a mirage
come on try please
I can see a beautiful city
another trick of the desert
the city forsaken
you have found a lake
a thing as empty as this city
as simple as water
will I tell you something

all this strikes me as interesting
a real lake
as lovely as getting wet
now you have convinced me
all & sundry stare at the stars
from there I always smile at you
you too smile back at them
I want to give you a beautiful gift
whatever is imagined will come true
this desert is very cold
where are you
in the future what things
what things I will tell you.

Translated by Neil P. Doherty

'Çöl' from *Dünya İnancı-Toplu Şiirleri*. Istanbul: Yapı Kredi Yayınları, 2012.

King's Crown

If, in this world, someone is shutting a window
 - knowing nothing of any place or time -
There is surely someone else getting him to do it.
As the stars glance at their symmetrical past
they steal a look too, at the King's crown.

The moon and the stars are but a small milieu, they say
 - we hold the seven colours of the spectrum in one
this simple wish has nothing to do with the dead -
yet this great silence does not take in the stars
that is attended to by one of those lowly ones.

And the servants in your eyes
Would like, just for a moment, to leave down their ironing

Translated by Neil P. Doherty

'Kral Tacı' from *Dünya İnancı-Toplu Şiirleri*. Istanbul: Yapı Kredi Yayınları, 2012.

The Falling

Under the falling leaves I am holding
a desert that cannot abide thirst.
(A desert, a desert...)
I am holding hold your ties
I'd love to know your time.

At midnight a gazelle is escaping from the garden
bringing her back will take years.
(Wilderness, wilderness...)
And years later that garden.

Warm bread waylays us now
I feel like I am going to see a rabbit
whenever I step out into the fields for a bit.
 - In both senses the guest has gone now -

(You'd grown used to the place, hadn't you?)

Before heading out on its travels
through houses
and doors
wanders a wind
like the last stirrings of pain
like the first samples of living,
however unfulfilled.

Weep, weep

Translated by Neil P. Doherty

Dökülen

Dökülen yapraklar altına tutuyorum
susuzluğa dayanamayan bir çöl.
(Çöl, çöl...)
Senin kravatlarını tutuyorum
bilmek istiyorum zamanını senin.

Bir ceylan kaçıyor bir bahçeden gece yarısı
onu geri getirmek yıllara malolacak.
(Yaban, yaban...)
O bahçe yıllar sonra…

Sıcak ekmek yolumuzu kesiyor artık
hep bir tavşan görecekmiş gibi oluyorum
Kırlara azıcık çıktığım zaman.
 - Her iki anlamda konuk artık gitmiş - .

(Alıştın buralara sen de)

Dolaşıyor çıkacağı yolculuktan önce
evleri
kapıları
bir rüzgar
acının gidişi gibi damlarda
ilk örnekleri gibi yaşamanın
doyamadan da olsa.

Ağla ağla

'Dökülen' from *Dünya İnancı-Toplu Şiirleri*. Istanbul: Yapı Kredi Yayınları, 2012.

Stove

Our rooms
were warm.
Like
people.

The weather cold.

And we were like
the cheap stoves
of our rooms.

The teapot
atop the
hot stove.

We'd burn poems
so our lovers
couldn't read
them.

The stoves of
the old world

Translated by Neil P. Doherty

'Soba' from *Dünya İnancı-Toplu Şiirleri*. Istanbul: Yapı Kredi Yayınları, 2012.

Gigi

Angel of invisible meetings Gigi,
how well we did getting the angels to listen to music,
the children are now embarrassed by their long ears
and the angels are asleep in the meadows Gigi
when they grow bored they measure out bird seed
though they do not sell it to the birds Gigi
in dust, in dirt, I dwell
but who is trying to remind the birds
that it is seed they eat
who is out working out in the meadows Gigi
perhaps it is the tailors of fairytales?

Like some fool I will die Gigi
like a fool hiding my love away from you
into a wall I'll bury you Gigi
you'll be invisible though people will see you
they know what I've seen Gigi
you wished for a broken doll in the garden
that wanted me to trip and fall
just don't tell of all the places I've been Gigi

Translated by Neil P. Doherty

'Gigi' from *Dünya İnancı-Toplu Şiirleri*. Istanbul: Yapı Kredi Yayınları, 2012.

Salih Aydemir (1967 -)

Salih Aydemir was born in Amasya in 1962. From 1990-97 he worked as journalist in Ankara. His poems appeared in various magazines throughout the 1990's before he began to bring out a magazine called *Öteki-siz* in 2000. In that same year his first book, a series of 'poetic experiments' entitled *(h)içlenmeler*, was published by İlgi Yayınevi. Since then he has published six books of poetry and a book of essays. Since the collection entitled *Dilbendi*, published by Şiirden Yayıncılık in 2009, he has been mining a rich field of elliptic, almost minimal poetry.

broken pen

songs leave a taste in the eyes of sleeping women
& so you will kiss their dreams before morning breaks
caressing 'now' like some broken pen

wherever you cry is where you'll grow old
forgetting every song you'd stored in your memory.

Translated by Neil P. Doherty

'Kırık Kalem' from *Gölge Göçü*. Şiirden Yayıncılık, 2014.

shakespeare

with the sun i am going down
into that sweet crackle of silence

leave a word for me
sustain the value of silver

emptiness
long time a knot

offer up
poppies that will trouble me

was it guilt
that changed anger
or anger by
the word

my pen abdicates
leave me out on the street

Translated by Neil P. Doherty

shakespeare

güneşle iniyorum
suskunluğun o tatlı hışırtısına

bana bir söz bırak
güç ver gümüşün değerine

boşluk
uzun zamandır düğüm

bana
dert olacak gelincikler sun

suç mu
değiştirdi öfkeyi
öfkeyi
yoksa söz mü

tahttan iniyor kalemim
beni sokakta bırak

'shakespeare' from *Dilbendi*. Şiirden Yayıncılık, 2009.

salt life

knowing
the secrets of locks
letters ground in the mills of the mind
in sweat the coyness of remaining a child

on palms the face turns
music, something else again

Translated by Neil P. Doherty

‘tuz ömrü’ from *Dilbendi*. Şiirden Yayıncılık, 2009.

since the long rains

madly the mornings   ooze into my feet
from the glances of distance the waterfaced women drizzle
their voices   a song of despair   in hand on tongue
Istanbul   like timid leaves the twig of a branch

since those long rains
i have hidden in a skin   child
if only you knew   just   how close to the poisons i am
if you knew - shall i say - that I'd lost the life i raised
but still keep far   away
a mortal tongue will kiss you for me

to the deafest days of time i left all my sleep
the night is slowly slowly dispersing   i am silent, am silent

silent

the answers wake after twelve, and look for their questions

Translated by Neil P. Doherty

'uzun yağmurlardan beri' from *Gölge Göçü*. Şiirden Yayıncılık, 2014.

Asuman Susam (1968 -)

Asuman Susam was born in Izmir and studied Turkish Language and Literature at Ege University. Her first poems appeared in *Milliyet Arts Magazine* in 1989, and the Young Poets Anthology of the same year. In addition to poetry, she also writes on literature and cinema, and her articles have appeared in various different magazines. Her most recent collection of poems is *Kemik İnadı*, published in 2015.

Sylvia

i'm just as sad as you, Sylvia
but i go on seeding suicide
to fall on my soil like rain
keeping my sweet-tempered herbs green

if my virgin word were torn apart
while every inch of me smells of dried blood
has my stitching up of the rent places in me
kept me speaking an unseen grief

Sisyphus loved the desert
ah, the oasis that proclaims the unknown
can punishment be a hopeless bliss
you couldn't bear the joyless hopes
is there an error in that
i saw
how illusory the summit was
plunging headlong
that joke between me and the void
don't conceal your smile, Sylvia
rehearsing to die is always a bit funny
once a gentleman critic
referring to me recalled you
saying i had a confessing poet-woman's hunger
something like latent diabetes, i guess
i confess i wasn't aware of it
we two actually have nothing in common
i've now grown used to exile
but maybe i should say
that in the sisterhood of the irascible and restless
we do share a few traits
having already begun let me say this too
i never liked
seeing myself in poetry's looking glass
If i'd been carried everywhere
by my lover's pocket-mirror

and when he kissed the fire on my forehead
i'd scattered like pomegranate seeds
 - if i'd, if i'd...
but no such things happened

in a daze now as if watching the milk boil over
i review everything i've learned by heart
clearly i don't fit into this bell-jar, Sylvia
as Galip's sky-blue asuman...she's different
i'm washing myself away
i can't be dim water's reflection
or some man's ophelia
not the shiver of his soul...
your blue is totally different

forgetting myself at a wellhead
i watch my childhood's seasons
everything i thought i couldn't remember
is a new story there...
i've dropped memory's string
i'm on smooth solid ground, Sylvia
this warning flare between my life and me
may only be some foolish revelry

Translated by Saliha Paker and Mel Kenne

'Sylvia' from *Kemik İnadı*. Istanbul: Can Yayınları, October 2015.

Gökçenur Ç (1971 -)

Gökçenur Ç was born in Istanbul in 1971 and still lives there. He has seven books of his own poetry and has translated selected books of poetry by Wallace Stevens, Paul Auster and Ursula K. Le Guin. He has participated in and/or organized poetry translation workshops and festivals in many countries. His poems have been translated into 25 languages and published in numerous magazines and anthologies in Italy, Bulgaria and Serbia as well as in Turkey. He is the prime mover and co-director of *Word Express* (www.word-express.org) and a founder and board member of Delta International Cultural Interactions Association. He edits the literary magazine, *Çevrimdışı İstanbul* (Offline İstanbul) and is a member of the international committee of *Voix de la Méditerranée* festival in Lodeve, France. He is also a member of the editorial board of the Macedonian-based international literary magazine, *Blesok*.

You're Far from Your Country, I Am in Your Country

You're far from your country, I am in your country
my poems are like letters that as time goes by
are lost in the mail:

You'd dozed off for a long while, on your banana yellow couch
your hair knot unravelled, your glasses falling, from your hand to the floor
four eaten apples out of five on the plate
a comb you placed between two pages of a book
on your knees a coverlet of prussian blue
in your dream maybe you are watching
a scene from the play Old Sounds

you're in my family's house, your mother has not gone insane yet
my brother isn't drafted
Zeki Müren is singing
'You Are Far Away'
on the radio
very soon stopping the song in the middle
they'll announce that the armed forces are taking over
'for the safety and security of the country'
very soon you will say
'I need to go' 'I can't come because Turkish is...'

A thousand times you watched this play
but for the first time, about to wake up soaking in sweat,
you'll notice a wrinkled telegram message
against the gramaphone on the stand:

. ./ 'don't ever wake up. ./ 'wind. ./'
like news from me. ./ 'on your breast a dry
 / 'leaf will drop. ./ '

You are far from your country, your country in chaos
this moment I'm alive
beloved still, in doubt, immune to separation

Translated by Murat Nemet-Nejat at the 2014 Cunda International
Workshop for Translators of Turkish Literature

'Ülkenden Uzaktasın, Ülkendeyim' from *Her Kitabın El Kitabı*. Istanbul: Yitik Ülke
Yayınları, 2007.

Sultry Summer Rains

The mountain across the sea - brightened by the fishing villages
burning at its feet - is swaying between your firm breasts like a
sleepy ruby necklace
You are singing a song that reminds me of a dream I saw, then forgot

*- A black cello case was floating on the steppe's yellow sea, yellow like
wheat ears waving in the wind. I catch hold of the case, open the lid
and crows fly up, covering the death-pale light of the sun -*

you say that every dream tells as much of death as life, before you
leap up with joy and chase a fire fly
this is how we are; we laugh with or without a reason
we are running naked through rice fields with the same quick shock
of a peasant that wakes up under a pear tree

petrified moonlight pierces the soles of our feet,
old longings are not so much as a silver splinter in the fingertip of love

we are hopeful, if this is what hopefulness is
we don't know where they go, the memories of the dead
but we ask ourselves each morning, thinking we're asking you
oh soul! - You lost oyster that rolls and grows the pearl of consciousness -
if birds flying backwards are a sign of good weather

I run and catch you as your voice leaves prints upon tall grasses
I say 'my beloved, my job and my poetry lie before me like three roads
and what a shame, for I would like to travel at least two of them'

Hush you say, the full moon is rising on our night like a lantern
within a drum
Remember, how we used to wet hands in the hollow of a tree, to cure them
Rose-coloured clods of earth hang in the air

the impulse that makes tired flowers turn to the new day
what is a root when it is not clinging?
perhaps the memories of our dead are sprinkled
on living hearts like sultry summer rains

We sit and talk of things that will never return
my mother, who brews up mint and senna
and those lovely old days when we kissed under the rain

Translated by Caroline Stockford at the 2014 Cunda International
Workshop for Translators of Turkish Literature

'Bungun Yaz Yağmurları' from *Söz'e Mezar*. Istanbul: Yitik Ülke Yayınları, 2010.

You Can't Go Up This Mountain with So Many Words on Your Back

What's this place, I asked, it's Ithaca, they said, don't get up,
                         you're tired, you're frozen,
with so many words on your back you can't go up this mountain.

They gave me some Ithaca brandy to drink, some Ithaca soup, a
                         hard bed to lie on and silence to think.

The monk-plum, green and sour, we also call it plum-of-blue-time
                         though its real name is the Ithaca plum,

it clears the mind, gives joy to words, they said,

when I got stuck on my lines they gave me new breath.

When the world scared me I hid away in books.

They gave me thick ones, a new name and some advice.

I'm good here, I said; this unbroken peace of mind

is the bliss of things that love their names, they said.

This is how I returned to Ithaca, of which I'd never heard, from which
                         I'd never departed.

Translated by Saliha Paker at the 2014 Cunda International Workshop for Translators of Turkish Literature

Sırtında Bunca Sözcükle Çıkılmaz Bu Dağa

1 – Burası neresi dedim, ithaka dediler, kalkma, yorgunsun, donmuşsun,
sırtında bunca sözcükle çıkılmaz bu dağa.

2 – İthaka rakısı, ithaka çorbası, sert bir döşek ve düşünecek sessizlik
verdiler bana.

3 – Keşiş erikleri, yeşil ve ekşi, mavi zaman eriği de deriz ama asıl adı
ithaka eriğidir, zihni açar, sözcükleri şenlendirir dediler, takıldığım
dizelerde bana esin verdiler.

4 – Dünyadan korkunca kitaplara saklanırdım.

5 – Kalın kitaplar, yeni bir ad, biraz akıl verdiler bana.

6 – Burada iyiyim dedim; bu geçmek bilmez erinç adını seven nesnelerin
esenliğidir dediler.

*7 – İşte böyle döndüm ithaka'ya, ne adını duymuştum, ne ithaka'dan
çıkmıştım yola.*

'Sırtında Bunca Sözcükle Çıkılmaz Bu Dağa' from *Sırtında Bunca Sözcükle Sırtın-
da Bunca Sözcükle*. Istanbul: Yitik Ülke Yayınları, 2012.

A Tartar Post-Rider Sleeps on His Horse

He said, 'I came by the first plane'.

(The wind was blowing like
God's unkept promise to the mountain.
A flock of birds rising up from the elderberry tree,
 perched on the roof of the house.)

They found him in the garden, under the pomegranate tree
flat on his face, over his typewriter, the woman said,
the lantern he'd hung on the branch was still burning,
and just there were two full buckets of milk,
with fallen pomegranate petals on top,
as if he'd just left the house to milk the sheep
and just as he was passing by the table, one last sentence had come
to mind that he wanted to get down before he forgot it.

On the table were nail clippers, pens, water bills,
unopened envelopes, the last issue of a poetry magazine,
a photograph of his mother, she is smiling, the days when cancer
would suck her marrow were still far off,
a black Remington typewriter, its keys stuck halfway
toward attacking the paper, bits and pieces of his glasses
among the letters: in the noon sun shards of diamonds,
a lament to the unfinished text: A sheet of paper,
blood splashed between the words________

He pulled the paper out as if he was pulling the sword he'd plunged
into the breast of an enemy.

(Voices were far away, visions were dipped into the mist of meaning-
lessness, the ground beneath his feet shifted, he grabbed the table's edge
and for the first time read something his father had written.)

'With the tools of the mind, you cannot encompass anything not
created by the mind. Madness is but a deviation of observation, not
an object of it. Eskimos can see sixteen different types of ice. Hindus

use the same word for both ice and snow. Some Indian tribes have
no word for time.

> Sumach turns red.
> On the plain the shadow of a cloud widens.
> The words we wanted to say for a long time
> Trickle down from the pomegranate leaves
> Like the first drops of rain,
> And drip onto the whiteness of the paper.

Hence, language is not only a tool of communication but at the
same time an act of classification and elimination. One day, I read a
sentence like, 'The sun was shining green'. I was seventeen. 'What can
this be?' I thought. I was seventeen. I was in love, and I was thinking
that rain had not stopped for fifteen days and I couldn't go out and
I had never seen the sun shining green. Because no one had ever
said, 'The sun is shining green'. I went out. I looked at the sun. It was
shining as green as fresh almonds.

> It rains on those who say it's raining and
> on those who don't say it's raining
> On the beet fields and on the sea,
> On the mountains and on the fishermen's nets,
> It rains on everything,
> And still everything is as dry as words

Forms are erected on the selected and discarded 'realities' of the
past. On facing a new reality that does not conform to those forms,
what we eliminate is not the form but that very reality. Seeing is not
believing; believing is seeing. Therefore, there must be a constant
conflict between concepts and reality. Concepts are like a Greek
statue that knelt down to draw his bow; realities are like a Tartar
mailman who sleeps on his horse: He keeps shooting the arrow,
not knowing where it will fall. The pomegranate tree in my garden
struggles ceaselessly with the concepts of being a tree and a pome-
granate tree. I call this the loss of being in the labyrinth of rain. Light
has forgotten the way out. Being an individual requires a battle with
the already conceptualized form of the individual. But this is a dan-
gerous thing to do. I saw a chicken slaughtered just because it fought

with the concept of chicken and therefore it didn't lay eggs. Is this
not the sacrifice of reality to the god of concepts?

> It rains on the branches of date trees and elderberries,
> On your shoulders and on the island mimosas,
> On deserted terraces, on your very short hair
> It rains on everything,
> Yet everything still looks like everything.

Lets go back to the beginning: The very language that performs the
task of selection and elimination is created by the collective mind.
The individual who wishes to see the invisible is either mad or mad.
I choose to be a poet instead of being mad. That's why they believe
that I'm mad. Because, although he doesn't change the method of
observation, the poet changes the language which is the sifter. I have
lived amongst them. I never forgot the wet green almonds. I wrote
about everything I saw. I would have liked to write about my own
death.'

They hugged each other and cried for their father
Whom they never hugged when he was alive.

Translated by Clifford Endres and Selhan Savcıgil Endres at the 2014
Cunda International Workshop for Translators of Turkish Literature

'At Üstünde Uyur Bir Posta Tatarı' from *Söz'e Mezar*. Istanbul: Yitik Ülke Yayınları, 2010.

Gonca Özmen (1982 -)

Gonca Özmen was born in Burdur, Turkey in 1982. She took her B.A. and M.A. degrees from the English Language and Literature Department of Istanbul University, where she is now studying for her PhD. Her first poem was published in 1997, and that year she was awarded the Yaşar Nabi Nayır Youth Prize and named 'a poet worth watching'. In 1999 she received the Ali Rıza Ertan Poetry Prize. In 2000 her first book of poetry *Kuytumda* (In My Nook) was published and won the Orhan Murat Arıburnu Poetry Prize. In 2003 Istanbul University honored her with the Berna Moran Poetry Prize, and in 2005 she won the Homeros Criticism Prize for an essay she wrote on the Turkish poet Edip Cansever. Her second book *Belki Sessiz* (Maybe Quiet) was published in February 2008. She has attended international conferences throughout Europe, and her poems have been translated into Spanish, French, English, German, Slovenian and Persian. *The Sea Within*, a selection of her poems translated by George Messo, was published by Shearsman Books in February 2011. She has been living in Istanbul since 2000.

Ruin

Sebastian there's nothing I can tell you about the snow of this mountain
Your every waking isn't splinters, your every turn is not beyond you
You've never given birth so how can you know
Being split down the middle not like a pomegranate or watermelon
It's not so easy to reach that spell
To gather your things and migrate to your own stomach
To become a ruin

Sebastian in the past I had red animals
Howling at night from both of us for both of us to both of us
If two of us love the same man will a rose grow from this
Let's take blue buses let's take them and be cooler
Let's listen to songs of pain and chew their fruit
My hanging in between
Would it be something my lover could see

Once I was in love with a rhinoceros
Once he looked at me
Once I had a lump in my throat
Once I was burning for him
Once I was stilled

Sebastian didn't you once lose your heart too

Translated by Zoë Skoulding and Gonca Özmen

'Mundar'

My Lamb

Said says revolution. My hair in a bun.
Said and I our mouths are half open. We breathe sounds in and out.
We believe in Sümeyra. My hair tied up.

To the one nestling beside him Said never says no. He says my lamb.
To the one nestling beside me I never say no.
Jar û Evin. Jar û Evin.

If I could find water, find water to cleanse myself
My hair tied up like this. Dull like this. Neat like this

They say my lamb to me - I say to them my lamb

I'm afraid when anyone says for you I will lay down my life
As I grow afraid, the bells of my body are jangled
As I grow afraid, goats are raucously mating

Said says massacre. My hair tied up.
Said and I our mouths are half open. We breathe deaths in and out.
We believe in Süleyman. My hair tied up.

If I could find a lover, find a lover to deceive me
My hair tied up like this. Mute like this. Half-light like this.

Translated by Zoë Skoulding and Gonca Özmen

'Kuzum,' *üç nokta*, Spring 2012.

Copper Bucket

Everyone lived in distances I was always calling
Everyone had another woman before me

I was stubborn, rough, a copper bucket swinging to and fro
In the cheerfulness of others I was clumsy

Those opened up by the wind in me
Those hanging from the sky's mind
What could I take from you, I left

Say if you like that I wandered in the hollows of trees
In every bush I darkened my destiny a little

However hard I tried I couldn't reach the wonder you believe in
Everyone's complete but I couldn't be

I stared like a child falling over
The world is a sinking place
I did not fly, I did not fly

Translated by Zoë Skoulding and Gonca Özmen

'Bakraç', *Kitap-lık*, January 2010.

Batuhan Dedde (1987 -)

121

Batuhan Dedde was born in Istanbul in 1987. He has published several books, including the poetry collection *Kırmızı Eroin* (*Tahta Putun Şiirleri*) in 2013. His work attempts to bring together the sensibilities of the American Beats and the Turkish Second New.

A Midsummer Night's Lucid Dream Left Over from Spring

The stars are so beautiful here,
salaam alaikum, Lord!

It was a summer night like this, warm and full of stars
when in this world I was a runaway child
but it turned out in time that humanity and goodness and mercy
were all a big scam
I had met a woman
timid yet brave
happy but broken
female but innocent
and a whole bunch of other adjectives...

I didn't have my eyes on her breasts but I fucked her dreams
I'm a lying
you're a lying
they're a lying son of a bitch
for the most part...
Even Pinocchios have hearts, babe!

So one night I boarded a ship from Platform 33
and that ship abandoned me to roads I could not escape from.
I traveled through darkness, along seashores, over mountains, etc.
A symphony of strings inside my head!
a cigarette of orgasm in the corner of my mouth
a smile like a massacre on my stupid face
I ran to whores without looking back at the wreckage that was piling
                                             up behind me...
Of all the bad men I have known, commander, quite of few have had
                                             hearts that were broken,
and other parts too, here and there, just like their lives.
And I have no heart, just a vagina. Which you can fuck at your leisure.
Don't you forget, O poet Cemal Süreya,
that even if you keep running after losing the race, it doesn't mean
                                             you're not defeated!

I exhibit behaviors that cause me pain
like a dirty dog
Where the hell are we, man?
Isn't there a single stop for light on this route of darkness?
Well then
let my blood spill in the warm wind on that dock
let my soul spill like small change
but only at the moment, right across from the dock
when I kiss your lips
I'm a wound and I've fallen far behind,
the scars erased from day to day.
I'm a few hours behind the human race
and in a little while I'll board a ship bound straight for hell
So fuck this motherfucking merry-go-round!

Allah, just blow my brains out.
            Amen.

Translated by Donny Smith

'Bahardan Kalma Bir Yaz Gecesi Lucid Rüyası' from *Kırmızı Eroin (Tahta Putun Şiirleri)*. İstanbul: Altıkırkbeş, 2013.

What Have You Carried Over? Poems of 42 Days and Other Works
Gülten Akın

Edited by Saliha Paker and Mel Kenne
Talisman House, Publishers, 2014 , $17.95

Does poetry have a social role to fulfill or is it simply a means for individual expression? This question drives the work of Gülten Akın (1933-2015), a poet whose work traverses the divide between the self and the other.

What Have You Carried Over? is a superb collection that includes selected translations from Akın's twelve volumes of poetry, including her important *Poems of 42 Days* in its entirety. The translations, the majority done by the editors, nicely capture the nuances of the Turkish and render difficult phrases accessible, striving for (and attaining) a fidelity to Akın's original.

Akın's deft handling of the personal and social can be seen in her first collection, *The Hour of Wind,* where a series of love poems celebrate both the intense joy and melancholic anxiety that love can bring. Akın's poems do a marvelous job of capturing this duality, reminding us how intertwined love is with the possibility of losing the beloved.

Social questions begin to appear in *The Red Carnation.* In a cycle of poems revolving around seasons, a blind 30-year-old woman laments the hard rural life of Anatolia. Akın is able to convey suffering through precise details like 'I know the potatoes of one summer's toil / Will not provide a piece of serge'. The next three poems discuss the murder of her son, the kidnapping of her daughter-in-law, and the fact that 'no one's got the time / To stop'n think about fine things'. Even though the series ends with 'the summer I love' the reader cannot help but feel the injustice of the situation.

Akın's *Poems of 42 Days* illustrates the tension between individual sorrow and collective suffering as she details the anguish of mothers petitioning for their sons' release from prison. 'The Yard' traces a mother's scream as it works its mysterious effects on the guards. Akın highlights the anguished individual as they temporarily step out of the group to make their feelings known. This tension between group solidarity and personal lament is captured in 'The Blonde Girl' where the speaker explains 'She wanted them to understand that each of them was one among many, yet each was a human being'. Akın's ability to convey the tension between the one and the many is perhaps the most interesting aspect of her work.

Akın's later poetry is less directly political but no less socially-engaged. In *Then I Grew Old*, Akın laments the loss of connectedness in today's world: 'no one can unite / with the metallic discourse of antennas and satellites'. This interest in what might be 'carried over' from one human to another reaches an existential climax in '*The Scene*': 'Is the eye in this happening / the seer or the seen / or has this I now become / the whole scene?' Ceaselessly exploring both her personal vision and its relation to the social, Akın's writing is an answer to this query.

Erik Mortenson

Garip

I translated the *Garip Manifesto* and the poems originally printed with it that appear here 20 years ago for a course I taught on poetry and politics in the Mediterranean but did not find a publisher then. The international status of Turkish literature has risen over the years, and I am glad for Turkish Poetry Today's invitation to contribute them to this issue.

Garip - 'Strange', was a movement started by the poetry three friends began to write as teenagers in the 1930s and collected in a slim volume of that name in 1941, prefaced with the manifesto written by Orhan Veli. He, Oktay Rıfat and Melih Cevdet were born at the outset of World War I and lived through the excitements and privations of the struggle for independence and the cultural revolution that followed the founding of the Republic, as well as the Nazi era that then loomed over Turkey, and World War II. They grew up in the neglected grace of cool, high-ceilinged buildings left by the Ottoman Empire and Le Corbusier-like cubic structures with flat roofs built in Ankara, where they met. They worked in government offices at relatively undemanding jobs given their talents, read French poetry and drank a lot of rakı. In the official story of the Republic, literature was a tool of nation building and the writer was the voice of the people. But the *Strangers* shrugged that off; they spoke for themselves.

What accounts for the ironic nonchalance that was their most apparent feature, and for many a maddening one? What made them refuse the earnest preoccupations that kept other poets repeating themselves with the drivel generations of schoolchildren would be forced to memorize (last I looked, such 'national poetry' was still a required field even for doctoral students in Turkish literature). How to write about war? How to praise Atatürk? How to raise the downtrodden and inspire them to embrace national identity? What to do with Ottoman divan poetry - should one use its courtly *aruz* meter, shared for centuries by Arabic, Persian, Ottoman and Urdu, or the *hece* meter of rural folk?

The *Strangers* wrote in free verse, established in modern Turkish most famously by Nâzım Hikmet, but also by Ahmet Haşim, whose intricate, Symbolist-seeming poetry the *Strangers* ridiculed. They ridiculed everyone except Nâzım, who read their work eagerly in his exile. Only Yahya Kemal would do interesting work with *aruz*, and in the next generation Cemal Süreya, default spokesman for the Second New, gave the title *Folklore is the Enemy of Poetry* to a collection of his wonderful essays.

The *Strangers* come in here: after the solitary titans Haşim and Yahya Kemal, born in the 1880s; and Nâzım, born in 1902; İlhan Berk, who was of *Garip's* time but tread the long, long arc of his own brilliant star, continuing past the late 1950s emergence of the Second New poets Cemal Süreya, Turgut Uyar, Edip Cansever, and Ece Ayhan (certain novelists should be counted too); as Oktay Rıfat and Melih Cevdet were striking out new paths.

The popularity of *Garip*, and Orhan Veli's poetry in particular, is remarkable. *Garip* created a giant sensation when it came out, and the posthumous 1951 edition of Orhan Veli's collected poems, which reprinted the manifesto, went through 57 editions by 1998. The book remains to be written about how the *Strangers*, nonchalantly, gave direction to the language revolution and made it a thing alive. For all this work was done while the Turkish language underwent the most radical change in the history of language - any language. True, the 1880s to 1930s were a time of linguistic change and control elsewhere as well, and one can point to failed and successful attempts at linguistic reform, but nothing in history approaches the radicalism of the Turkish revolution in language.

To return to my question of what made the *Strangers* so independent, everything they wrote is evidence that they worked this thing through for themselves. There is a kind of chicken or the egg essentialist tradition in literary criticism that puts great stock in belatedness and influence. One of the odd things about it is how it assumes that being conversant with methods and styles coming from outside one's own country is something that requires an accounting, and even a compromise of one's integrity, as if only the near-at-hand can be genuine. This seems to be the other side of the 'national poetry' coin, although it is true that Ottoman poets were once preoccupied with *tetebbu*, intellectual apprenticeship (reappearing in today's political discourse as 'tutelage'). But that discussion does not tell us about poetry.

Orhan Veli begins his Manifesto by referring allusively to the situation immediately around him, and then moves on to the international scene as he criticizes artificiality in concrete detail. His central theme is purity. 'Pure poetry' was the great theme of Ottoman poets. For them it was poetry whose ultimate source was God. For the *Strangers* and most moderns, the unconscious was the infinitely original source. Meter and rhyme must be discarded because they have no place there, and therefore, too, no set vocabulary can be 'poetic' in itself. Surrealism may be the definitively modern movement in its belief in the unconscious, although automatism is merely a starting point. Art is mimesis, and the imitation is of the unconscious.

Victoria Rowe Holbrook

***

Editorial Note: The following translation of The *Garip* Manifesto is not the first rendering into English of this important document, even though when Victoria Rowe Holbrook queried us about including her version of it in *Turkish Poetry Today*, we all (including Victoria) thought it was. We only later discovered that at least one other English translation of it was extant, produced by Sidney Wade and Efe Murad and published on November 8, 2015, in the online journal *The Critical Flame* (www.criticalflame.org/garip-a-turkish-poetry-manifesto-1941). While we at first questioned the value of publishing another translation of the work, as we read and studied both translations and concluded that each was true to the intentions of the original and quite good in its own right, we also felt that certain differences in style and the interpretation of a number of nuances in words and phrases by the translators justified the publication of another rendering of it. In any case, two published versions of such an influential work can only add to the richness of Turkish literary scholarship and further aid researchers in the field of modern Turkish poetics.

Orhan Veli

Strange
Thoughts on Poetry
and
Selected Poems of Melih Cevdet, Oktay Rifat and Orhan Veli, 1941

The art of poetry has undergone many changes over the centuries to finally arrive at the point where it is today. One must accept that poetry is now something quite different from plain speech. I mean that poetry as it is today presents itself apart from natural and everyday speech, exhibiting a relative strangeness. But the fine thing is that as a result of many daring efforts, this poetry has made itself accepted; it has established a tradition and done away with that aforementioned oddity. This is where the young person educated by today's intellectuals finds himself. Seeking poetry within the confines of what he has been taught, he assumes that poems born of a desire to sound natural must be natural. What needs to be pointed out to him is the relativity of this point of view, so that he may doubt what he has learned.

*

Tradition has kept poetry within the framework we call prosody. The principal elements of prosody are meter and rhyme. People first used rhyme so that the next line would be easily remembered, that is, as an aid to memory merely. But later they discovered a beauty in it. They considered the use of prosody, along with meter, which exists for more or less the same purpose, an art. And at the source of poetry there is this desire for play, as in the other arts. This desire had a notable importance for primitive man. But humanity has evolved much since then. People today - so I imagine and I hope - do not find in the use of meter and rhyme a power that leaves them in awe, or a beauty that brings them great thrills. And so those who have recognized this uncomfortable truth have come to regard meter and rhyme as the ancestors of a new poetic element called 'concordia' and have embraced this new blessing with all enthusiasm. If there is such a thing in a poem as a concordia that should be appreciated,

129

it is not achieved through meter or rhyme. Concordia exists apart from meter and rhyme, and in spite of meter and rhyme. But what makes it consciously felt in poetry, and informs even those who barely understand that concordia is present, is meter and rhyme. It is doubtless the most glorious naiveté to be capable of deriving pleasure from a concordia sensed in this way - achieved through meter and rhyme - or to think that saying anything in these primitive measures is art. As for the belief in another kind of concordia, I will explain later how unnecessary, even detrimental it is to poetry.

*

Let us also accept that, whatever else, meter and rhyme are constraints. They govern the poet's thought and sensitivity just as they bring about alterations in linguistic form. The grammatical oddities of metrical language are born of the strictures of meter and rhyme. Perhaps these oddities have been beneficial to poetry as well, in so far as they once expanded the means of expression. They might even be made principal virtues, apart from the concerns of versification. But this institution of verse has given some the notion that there is a 'structure special to poetic language'. They reject some poetry because 'it is like common speech'. This view, derived from meter and rhyme, will always find poetry that seeks its true course relatively strange and will never want to accept it.

*

The arts of speech and meaning often make use of those faculties of mind that alter and destroy the natural state of things. For man, who owes his knowledge and education to past centuries, nothing could be more natural. Simile is the power to see things as other than they are. Someone who does this is not considered odd, he is not accused of having done something unnatural. But today's intellectual regards those who avoid simile and metaphor, who describe what they see with words we all use, as 'strange'. His error is to take as his starting point a poetic sensibility arrived at by way of various deviations. Since the day writing first appeared, hundreds of thousands of poets have come forward, and each one has struck thousands of similes. What, I wonder, will the people we admire achieve by contributing a few more to literature? Simile, metaphor, hyperbole - and the richness of imagery produced by their combination - have, I hope, at last sated history's gaping maw.

*

In the history of literature there have been a great many changes in form and in every case a new form was regarded as a little strange and later accepted with ease. The kind of change accepted with difficulty is one in taste. We see that such changes occur rarely; furthermore, in literatures that emerge through such change there is an aspect that in spite of everything does not change, that continues to endure and is common to them all. In poetry that has to this day done nothing but serve the bourgeoisie, or before the industrial revolution, slaved away for religion and the feudal class, this unchanging aspect discloses itself as 'having addressed the taste of the well-to-do classes'. Those who had no such need to work for a living made up the well-do-to classes, and it is they who were the rulers of times past. The poetry that represented those classes achieved a perfection greater than it deserved. But the taste upon which the new poetry will be based is no longer the taste of that minority class. The people who fill the world today discover their right to live only at the end of perpetual strife. Poetry too is their right, like everything else, and it will address their taste. And this does not mean trying to use the old poetry's instruments to explain what the masses we are speaking of want. The problem is not to defend the needs of a class of people, but simply to seek out and find its sensibility, and make it dominant in art.

A new sensibility can only be achieved through new ways and new means. There is no new artistic move in stuffing the contents of this or that ideology into known forms. The structure must be changed from the foundation up. In order to free ourselves from the dulling, suffocating effects of the literature that has for so many years dominated, dictated and formed our taste and will, we must throw out everything that literature taught us. And if possible throw out even the language that threatens our creative activity with the notion 'one must think with this vocabulary when writing poetry'. Only in this way will we free ourselves of the habits that drive us to unnatural aberrations, and return to our purity and our truth.

The people history remembers favorably are always those who reside at its turning points. They destroy one tradition and establish a new one. More precisely, what they establish is a new system of constraints that comes from within. It becomes tradition only after being transmitted to future generations. The great artist is surrounded by endless constraints. But they are never laid down by his predecessors. He is a man who seeks more than what books teach, who works to impose new constraints upon art. The classicism of 17th-century France was restrictive but it was not traditional. For it introduced its own constraints. Although the writers of the 18th century were more traditional, their artistry did not rise to the level of founding a tradition. For their constraints were learned, not felt. One may feel either the necessity or the superfluity of a thing, but one must feel it. Those who feel the necessity are founders, and those who feel the superfluity are the demolishers. Both are more beneficial to the intellectual life of societies than those who continue a tradition. They may not always succeed. Whether or not their work abides is a matter of its relationship to alterations in the social structure and the importance of these alterations. Another reason for lack of success is the fact that doing is different from knowing what should be done. A person may not be able to perfect what he has built, but he may leave a valuable foundation to those who immediately follow him. Either he points out a way or says that a certain way is wrong. In other words, he may be the standard-bearer of a cause, its common soldier or its sacrifice. A person willing to sacrifice himself for the sake of an idea should be regarded with appreciation and gratitude. At the same time, a person willing to sacrifice himself has no need of appreciation and encouragement, for these will add nothing to his conviction. Just as they will subtract nothing from the audacity of the most profoundly reactionary movements...

*

I am not in favor of mixing the arts. One should take poetry as poetry, painting as painting, and music as music. Every art has its own special characteristics and means of expression. To express one's aim by these means while remaining confined within these characteristics is to respect the true values of art and allow for a particular effort, a certain labor. This is the work by which the beautiful is achieved. Music in poetry, painting in music, and literature in painting are nothing but tricks to which those who cannot surmount this challenge resort. Furthermore, when the arts penetrate into one another they lose much of their true value. For example, can one feel anything but scorn for the musicality produced by placing a few concordant words side by side in a poem when one compares it with the melodic variation and rich harmony of true music, which is a magnificent art? The 'simulacrum concordia' achieved by lining up assonant letters is that simplistic and base a trick. It is my opinion that the pleasure felt in such artifice derives from a sense of satisfaction at perceiving that concordia in poetry. Someone feels satisfaction when he understands something he supposes to be incomprehensible. For a person to assume that his satisfaction is the same thing as the success of the supposedly incomprehensible work is nothing more than for him to count himself equal to its author; in other words, it is born of his desire for self-regard. Thus the works people most love are those most easily understood. People who have only recently begun to develop a taste in music listen with awe to Tchaikovsky's *1812 Overture*, a work whose subject is taken from Napoleon's Moscow campaign, and which represents events as if in narrative painting. In the same way such people find Saint-Saëns's greatest work to be his *Danse Macabre*, which describes the dancing of corpses risen from their graves after midnight, the crowing of cocks at dawn and the return of the skeletons to their graves; and that of Borodin, his *On the Asian Steppes*, in which the progress of a caravan is represented with sounds of flowing water and the tinkling of bells. For a composer, in an art with means of expression as extraordinarily broad as music, to resort to such a simplistic trick as narrative representation is a defect too great to ignore. No great artist should exploit that sense of satisfaction derived from the type of inferiority complex I described above. The artist is required to discover the special characteristics of the art to which he has devoted himself and to show his skill in these characteristics. Poetry is an art of words the entire quality of which is in its style. That is to say it consists entirely of meaning. Meaning addresses man's psyche, not his five senses. Thus we should not forget that auxiliary chicanery like music, etc., will distract our attention from the true poetic element that directly addresses the human psyche and whose entire value resides in its meaning. People object to décor in theater, where it is so much more essential, yet they don't object to music in poetry.

Apollinaire, in his book titled *Calligrammes*, inserts another art into poetry: painting. For example, in a poem about rain he arranges the lines from the upper to the lower corner of the page. Similarly, in the same book he has a poem about a journey; the arrangement of letters and words draws before our eyes a picture made up of train cars, telephone poles, the moon and stars. If confession is necessary, it should be said that all this imparts to us the air of rain falling, and of a journey; Apollinaire does, with a bunch of tricks belonging to another art, put us into the atmosphere of the poetry.

Apollinaire is not the only one to have resorted to such tricks. There are many who insert pictures into poetry by using shape. Japanese poets, for example, often illustrated their topics with forms resembling reeds, lakes, moonlight, boats with sails of rush matting, and plum trees in bloom. Haşim used to find it magical that the word 'flame' as written in the old letters, reminded one of a real flame. I recount these examples one by one in order to explain that poetry can make use of painting just as it can of music.

Why shouldn't a poet who accepts the use of music also think of using painting, and if one goes further, even sculpture and architecture in his work? The fact is that even painting does not have the right to make use of sculpture. I imagine that Picasso, who for a while tried to make painting three-dimensional, has today realized his error. But close attention reveals that the examples I have given bring us to consider only the aspect of painting inserted into poetry that has to do with shape. Such poetry has not yet gained enough supporters and importance to be a problem. However, there are also poets who insert painting into poetry in the form of meaning, and crowds of people who support these poets. They have no difficulty counting as poetry writings the entire virtue of which consists in representation. In fact one should not accept these writings as poetry. As long as those who defend this point of view do not expand much on it, their ideas seem almost reasonable. We feel like giving them their due. We suppose that depiction is among the arts of poetry, and that every poem is more or less descriptive. This error comes of the fact that language is poetry's means of expression. Words, which are language's parts, are symbols, either directly of things in the world or of our thoughts. To evolved man, abstract thoughts appear to have no connection with the outer world. But the creature called man has a tendency to concretize even the most abstract thoughts, that is, he always tends to refer them back to matter, to objects.

Thus one should consider it natural that the art which emerges when words come together will also bring many objects before our eyes as well. But while considering this natural, one should never reach the conclusion that the entire capital of poetry is derived from the world brought to mind by these words, or that its entire value consists in the beauty of this world. Representation may be found in poetry. But representation - even if filtered through the lens of perception completely individual to the artist - should not be the fundamental element of poetry. What makes poetry poetry is the special characteristic in its style alone, and this is proper to meaning.

As the French poet Paul Eluard said, 'A day will come when literature is read only with the head, and it will attain a new life'.

*

Every new movement in literary history has brought to poetry a new frontier. It fell to us to expand that frontier to the maximum, more precisely, to rescue poetry from frontiers.

Oktay Rıfat tries in one of his letters to explain this idea by means of the concept of a literary school. He says: 'The idea of a school represents an interruption, a stance in time. It is adverse to speed and motion. The only literary movement that goes with the flow of life, that is not adverse to the dialectique mind, is the school-less movement'.

But can the quality of frontierlessness or schoollessness exist in poetry by itself, independently? Surely not. It should be considered natural that this quality brings a person to discover many new territories and enriches poetry with much plunder. By our reckoning, chief among the riches we have gathered on this frontier-expanding campaign are purity and simplicity. The desire to derive poetic beauty from these has driven us to contemplate more closely a realm which is poetry's greatest treasury, and stirs up a person in every stage of his life. That realm is the unconscious. Only there can nature be found in a state unaltered by the intervention of intellect. There the human soul exists in all its intricacy, with all its complexes, but in a raw and primitive state. It is this intricacy that is one of the characteristics of primitiveness and simplicity. We encounter feelings and impulses as abstractions only in books of psychology. Thus a poet who tries to write a poem about, say, lust, or a writer who fills pages in order to explain the vile, drives us away from life and reality. We find purity and simplicity in our childhood memories with the same richness, the same intricacy, and the same hatred of the abstract. Images of God as an old man with a beard, *jinn* as red dwarfs and fairies as girls in white robes show that the uncontaminated mind of the child has no patience for abstract thought.

I do not want 'the operation of intervening in the unconscious in order to find poetry in the pure and simple state' to be confused with the *symboliste* theory of plucking certain strings hidden within us, or that of Valéry, who described the creative process as 'being other than conscious'. In this matter the artistic movement that most closely approaches our desire has been *surréalisme*. These people, who made psychic automatism the point of departure for their system of thought and understanding of art, were forced to discard meter and rhyme. This necessity is also obvious to anyone who sees that psychic automatism and intellectual chicanery are irreconcilable things. The surrealists, who made it clear that one must choose between them, and did not hesitate to sacrifice these petty chicaneries for the sake of 'a poetry whose entire value is in its meaning' are certainly worthy of admiration'.*

The concept of automatism, which we find right in part, has in our country been considered to precisely define this school. But one should recall that it is only a point of departure. Here I should also add that, both for us and them, the operation of 'discharging the unconscious' regarded as the essential *fonction* of poetry, is not always accompanied by a state of trance. If that were the case, every

---

* It must be because we have mentioned *surréalisme* with this kind of sympathy now and then - or because they have not read *surréalisme*, or have not read our poetry - that some people describe us with this label when they write about our work. But just as we have no connection with *surréalisme* beyond the points in common I have discussed here, we are not related to any literary school.

one would be an artist. The artist, however, is someone able to use an acquired faculty outside of dream and related states. His value and stature are measured according to the skill with which he gains and uses that faculty. Breton, himself a doctor well familiar with Freud and a poet whose art and thought were concordant, said years ago that a consciousness acquired by practice can give a person the ability to excavate the well we call the unconscious.

But what is this ability? Consciousness is always - more or less - present in the act of putting psychic life into written form. In other words it would be impossible to put the unconscious into written form under normal conditions. So wouldn't it be counted a completely useless effort to try and make this impossible state a faculty? It is definitely not the faculty of discharging the unconscious. At most it could be the faculty of imitating the unconscious. What kinds of characteristics do the contents of the unconscious present? An artist is much better able to feel that, and feel it much more profoundly, than a man of science. As for his work, it is nothing but the imitation of this sense. The artist is an excellent mimic.

The master artist appears not to be a mimic. For the thing he imitates is original. The nature the realist writers of the 19th century described is not original. It was imitated by means of intellect. For that reason the work is a copy of a copy. It is when simplicity and primitiveness point to realities that they should become the capital of art also. For both bring true beauty to the work of art. A good artist imitates them beautifully. One should not say he is 'a simple, primitive person'. If a poet who has endured the trials of art for years and surmounted its endless stages appears before you one day with an inexperienced style, don't rush to negative conclusions. Such a poet may have found 'imitation of the primitive' beautiful. If so, it means he has become a master of that inexperience.

All this goes to show that art is not so much a matter of automatism, etc., but the work of effort and skill. A little earlier, however, while discussing *surréaliste* poets, I said 'these people, who made psychic automatism the point of departure for their system of thought and understanding of art, were forced to discard meter and rhyme'. So if they do not believe in such automatism, and can show that the entire effort is a matter of imitation, let them accept meter and rhyme as well. This observation might have been correct if what required the removal of meter and rhyme was solely its connection with the concept of automatism. But there are other reasons for devaluing meter and rhyme as well. For the time being I consider those reasons to be beyond the scope of the discussion.

I said that if what required the removal of meter and rhyme were solely its connection with the concept of automatism, then once this connection is understood to be unnecessary, meter and rhyme should reclaim their stature in poetry. But they should not. For the surréalist poets wanted the unconscious they inserted into poetry by way of imitation to seem real. So they were forced not to use meter and rhyme. For they were people who realized that it is not enough to know the thing to be imitated, one must also be a master of imitation. If this were not the case, we would not have believed they were sincere. The artist is also someone who convinces us that what he says is sincere.

*

Another thing I believe should be attacked in poetry is the mentality of the single line. This manifests itself in the form of the belief that it is sufficient for a poem to contain one single elegant line, and at first glance appears a simple matter but is significant because it is the hidden expression of fidelity to an inferior quality in poetry. Even those who believe a poem must exist as a 'whole' accept the principle of intervals between verses and consider the relations of meaning that tie them together sufficient for the perfection of the weave of a poem. This view is perhaps not so faulty as to be worthy of attack. But because it exposes a person to the danger of the characteristic I will now discuss, and leads to the taking of pleasure in it, one should give it no quarter either. A poem is such a totality that one never notices its wholeness.

We cannot see the mortar between the bricks in a building once it has been plastered and painted. It is only when the totality of the building has been achieved by means of this mortar that we have the opportunity to see the individual bricks that make it up and consider their qualities.

The single-line mentality allows us to scrutinize and analyze the lines and the words that are the pieces out of which they are made. Focusing on individual words, trying to ascertain their beauty or ugliness, has brought about the idea of the word as an abstract 'poetic element'. There are people who seek a hundred beauties in a hundred-word poem. But the fact is that even a thousand-word poem is written for the sake of one beautiful whole. Bricks are not beautiful. Plaster is not beautiful. But the work of architecture they make up is beautiful.Alternatively, let us suppose that a building could be made of materials like agate, bloodstone, and silver. If this building had no beauty other than the beauty of its materials, it would not be considered a work of art. Clearly, to take a word that is beautiful in as material for a poem does not add anything to it. Such words would do no harm if they did not bring their own style, usage, and forms along with them. But unfortunately these words can only be used in established ways; they themselves dictate their own style. Here we have the characteristic of the old poetry I mentioned above, and its style is called 'poetic'.

It was words that brought us to this style. But people who acquire their taste in poetry and their view of poetry from the society of today often start out at the other end, coming to know the poetic before they know those words. The vocabulary of words that can bring on this style automatically appears in the minds of people who want to be poetic when they write and seek the poetic when they read. It is impossible to escape the poetic without escaping the atmosphere of that vocabulary's atmosphere. The effort to bring a new vocabulary to poetry is manifestation of a desire for this liberation. Those who cannot stomach the use in poetry of the terms 'corn' and 'Süleyman Efendi' are those who can bear the poetic, even seek it, and seek it in particular.

But 'one should oppose everything belonging to the old, and above all the poetic style'.

Translated by Victoria Rowe Holbrook

139

Oktay Rifat and Orhan Veli

Bird with Cloud

Uncle Bird Keeper!
We have our bird too,
And our tree.
Just give us clouds
Ten cents worth.

'Kuş ve Bulut'

Melih Cevdet

from *Poems of Happiness*

II

When you are not in my poems
Why can't I finish them?
My heart, my heart, my heart;
How hard it is for you find what you search for!

(*Varlık No. 106*)

Harmonica

Last night as I went to bed
Someone passed by the house
Playing a harmonica
And it reminded me
Of the grill we lit in the evening
In my childhood
At the garden gate
Of our house by the Credit Union

'Ağız Mızıkası' (*Varlık, no. 109*)

from *Travel Poems*

I

One time I
On a very long train trip
Couldn't sleep,
Thinking of my bed at home
Tonight why can't I sleep
In my bed at home?

(*Varlık No. 104*)

from *Our Days*

Getting Up

In the old days when my grandmother
Got up to wash for morning prayers
Who was passing by in the street?
It was at a time like that I felt
Someone I loved had died.
Now in my memory there is only a name.
And the bitter factory whistle
That wakes up before everything.

'Kalkmak'

Living

On the back balconies I see from the streets I walk
Swing women's washed linen.
In the evening, when we meet along the river,
My lover smells of soap.

'Yaşamak' (*Varlık No. 107*)

Oktay Rifat

Thanks Be

I should thank
My buttoned boots and overcoat.
I should thank the falling snow,
This day, this gladness...
Thanks that my feet touch ground;
Thanks, to sky and earth;
To stars I don't know the names of,
Praise be to water and fire!

'Şükür' (*Varlık No. 158*)

Awe

How beautiful that hair doesn't go past the neck,
That it stops at our brow;
That eyelashes are one by one,
Eyebrows strand by strand!
How beautiful the human face,
Adam's apple and ten fingers!
And our world... All of these seasons,
Clouds, silvery poplars and Istanbul!

'Hayranlık'

Bread and Stars

The bread is on my knee
The stars far away, far far away.
I'm eating bread while I look at stars.
I'm so distracted that—don't ask,
Sometimes confused, instead of bread
I'm eating stars.

'Ekmek ve Yıldızlar' (*Ses No. 8*)

The Youth

He died, and doesn't know he died
His two hands testify; they're going to take him away,
He can't say I won't go.
He never tasted helva or sweets,
He couldn't thank even once
The friends who carried his bier
Oh, his death is not like anyone's!

'Sübyan' (*Varlık No. 154*)

Manifestation

What is this trial of mine!
I can't add
I'm an accountant.
My favorite dish is aubergine
It gives me indigestion.
I know a girl with freckles
I love her
She doesn't love me.

'Tecelli'

Orhan Veli

My Ships

On the pages of my schoolbook
My ships, my sailing ships.
They go to the land of the cannibals
My ships, heeling, heeling.
My ships, drawn with pencil;
My ships, with red flags.
On the pages of my schoolbook
Leander's tower,
And my ships.

'Gemilerim' (*Varlık No. 161*)

Robinson

My lady nanny is the most loved
Of my childhood friends
Since the day we wondered how to save
Poor Robinson from the lonely island
And wept together
At what hapless Gulliver
Suffered
In the land of the giants.

'Robenson' (*Varlık, No. 107*)

Headache

I

No matter how beautiful the journey
No matter how cool the night
The body tires,
A headache never does.

II

Now even if I go home
I might go out a little later
Since these clothes and shoes are mine
And since streets belong to no one.

'Baş Ağrısı' (*İnsan* No. 5)

I Can't Explain   (moro romantico)

If I cry, will you hear me,
In my verses;
Are you able to touch
My tears, with your hands?

I never knew songs were so beautiful,
Or words so lacking
Before I suffered like this.

There is a place, I know;
It's possible to say everything;
I've come pretty close to it, I feel it;
I can't explain.

'Anlatamıyorum'

Epitaph

He didn't suffer from anything in the world
As much as he suffered from corns.
Even being created ugly
Didn't affect him as much.
At times when his shoes didn't hurt
He didn't pronounce God's name but
He wasn't counted a sinner either.
It wasn't fair on Süleyman efendi.

'Kitabe-i Seng-i Mezar' (*İnsan* No. 5)

Oktay Rifat and Orhan Veli

Farewell Gathering

Tree

I threw a stone at a tree;
My stone didn't fall,
My stone didn't fall.
The tree ate my stone;
I want my stone,
I want my stone!

'Ağaç' (*Varlık No. 101*)

Contributors

ARZU AKBATUR holds a PhD. in Translation Studies from Boğaziçi University (Istanbul) with her dissertation entitled 'Writing/Translating in/to English: The 'Ambivalent' Case of Elif Shafak' (2011). She received her B.A. and M.A. degrees in English Language and Literature from Boğaziçi University and Yeditepe University (Istanbul) respectively. She is currently a lecturer in the Department of Translation and Interpreting Studies of Boğaziçi University, where she teaches Introduction to Translation, Translation Theories, Translation Criticism, and Literary Translation. Her main research interests include literary translation, Turkish Literature in English translation, translation and representation, translation and cultural identity. She has been a member of the steering committee of Cunda International Workshop for Translators of Turkish Literature (CIWTTL) since 2014.

JOHN ANGLISS is a professional literary and technical translator from Turkish to English. He has experience translating a wide range of literature, from poetry and drama to novels and short stories. Most recently, he translated Ekrem Eylisli's short story 'The Polecat' from Azeri Turkish for *Index on Censorship* together with Denis Ferhatovic. In collaboration with Maureen Freely, he translated the novels *Reckless* and *Shadowless* by Hasan Ali Toptaş. In 2011, he was awarded the British Council Turkey Young Translator's Prose Prize, while *Reckless* won a 2014 Pen Translates award. He lives in Ankara with his two cats, Tomris and Bihter.

GÖKÇENUR Ç was born in Istanbul in 1971 and still lives there. He has seven poetry books of his own and has translated selected books of poetry by Wallace Stevens, Paul Auster and Ursula K. Le Guin. He has participated in and/or organized poetry translation workshops and festivals in many countries. His poems have been translated into 25 languages and published in numerous magazines and anthologies in Italy, Bulgaria and Serbia as well as in Turkey. He is the prime mover and co-director of Word Express (**www.word-express.org**) and a founder and board member of Delta International Cultural Interactions Association. He edits the literary magazine, *Çevrimdışı İstanbul*, (Offline İstanbul) and is a member of the international committee of *Voix de la Méditerranée* festival in Lodeve, France. He is also a member of the editorial board of the Macedonian- based international literary magazine *Blesok*.

RUTH CHRISTIE was born and educated in Scotland, taking a degree in English language and literature at St Andrew's University. Later she studied Turkish language and literature at SOAS in London. Since 1993 she has translated much Turkish fiction and poetry into English, including collaborations with Richard McKane on collections of Nâzım Hikmet and Oktay Rifat. More recently her translation of Bejan Matur's *How Abraham Abandoned Me* was awarded the Poetry Book Society's Recommendation for 2012.

NEIL P. DOHERTY is a translator born in Dublin, Ireland in 1972 who has resided in Istanbul since 1995. He holds an M. Phil in Linguistics from Trinity College, Dublin, and currently teaches EAP to first-year students of psychology in Bilgi University. He is a freelance translator of both Turkish and Irish poetry and for the past few years has been somewhat quixotically endeavouring to assemble an anthology of modern Turkish poetry. He is also currently editing a volume of translations of Gökçenur Ç's work and translating a selection of the poetry of Metin Cengiz.

NILGÜN DUNGAN is a lecturer and a translator, based in the beautiful Aegean coastal town of Izmir, Turkey. She studied English Language and Literature at Ege University and received her master's degree in Administrative Management at Bowie State University. She is currently pursuing her PhD in Translation Studies at Bogazici University and teaches at Izmir University of Economics, the Department of English Translation and Interpretation. She has been a participant of the Cunda International Workshop for Translators of Turkish Literature since 2007 and translates Turkish fiction and poetry into English.

Clifford Endres has taught at the University of Texas at Austin and in Turkey at Ege, Boğaziçi, Başkent, and Kadir Has University. He is the author of the first book on *Austin City Limits* (1987) and has co-translated (with Saliha Paker and Selhan Savcigil-Endres) Turkish poets Enis Batur, Güven Turan, Gülten Akın, and novelist Selçuk Altun. These have appeared in *Agenda, Chicago Review, Edinburgh Review, Massachusetts Review, Near East Review, Quarterly West, Renaissance Quarterly, Seneca Review, Southwest Review,* and *Texas Studies in Language and Literature.*

Selhan Savcigil-Endres has taught at Hacettepe, Başkent, and Kadir Has universities and has written on Turkish and American authors such as Orhan Pamuk, Toni Morrison, and Paul Auster. Her translations (with Clifford Endres) of poetry and drama have appeared in, among others, *An Anthology of Modern Turkish Drama, New European Poets, The Massachusetts Review, Near East Review, Quarterly West, Seneca Review, Talisman,* and *Translation Review.* Translations of two novels by Selçuk Altun, *Many and Many a Year Ago* and *The Sultan of Byzantium,* were published respectively in 2009 and 2012.

Yusuf Eradam is the author of 13 books of his own, and 7 of translations. In 2011, he won the best translation award presented by the Ankara Art Foundation for his translation of *The Pillowman* by Martin McDonagh. He has also translated two Paul Auster novels, Herman Melville's masterpiece *Bartleby, the Scrivener* Sylvia Plath's *Ariel Poems*, and Gabards's *Psychiatry and the Cinema*. In 2008 he received a scholarship from the Writers Union of Sweden and represented Turkey in the first Baltic Congress with 600 other writers and translators from around the world. He has edited and contributed to many international and Turkish anthologies and has held five photography exhibitions. At present he lives and writes in Cihangir, Istanbul, while teaching American literature, cinema & popular culture at BAU.

Alev Ersan has worked collaboratively producing animation and performance works in Vancouver and Istanbul. Her writing has been published in *CanLit, FRONT* and *Morality In Fragments*. Her translations include *Automated Alice* by Jeff Noon (Postiga Press 2010) and shorter works by Birgül Oğuz, and Mine Söğüt. She currently teaches at Boğaziçi University and Kadir Has University.

VICTORIA ROWE HOLBROOK is author of *The Unreadable Shores of Love: Turkish Modernity and Mystic Romance* and translator of many Turkish works, among them *Beauty and Love* by Şeyh Galip, *The White Castle* by Orhan Pamuk, *The New Cultural Climate in Turkey: Living in a Shop Window* by Nurdan Gürbilek, *Listen: Commentary on the Spiritual Couplets of Mevlana Rumi* by Kenan Rifai, and *Playing with Violence: Violence in Contemporary Turkish Theater* by Esen Çamurdan.

İDIL KARACADAĞ was born in Istanbul in 1991. She acquired her BA in Literature at Kadir Has University and spent a year at Bath Spa University, England as an exchange student. She participated in the Cunda International Workshop for Translators of Turkish Literature in 2010, 2013, 2014 and 2015. She has translated various contemporary Turkish poets into English, and co-translated, with Mel Kenne, two novels and a novella by Zülfü Livaneli. Her translations have been published in *Turkish Poetry Today* and in the collection of Cunda translations, *Aeolian Visions/Versions: Modern Classics and New Writing from Turkey*, from the Cunda International Workshop for Translators of Turkish Literature, 2006-2012 (Milet Publishing 2013).

MEL KENNE is a poet and translator whose most recent books of poetry are *Take* (Muse-Pie 2011) and *Galata'dan/The View from Galata* (Yapı Kredi Yayınları 2010). A founding member of the Cunda Workshop for Translators of Turkish Literature, he has translated much Turkish poetry and fiction into English and was chief editor of *Aeolian Visions/Versions: Modern Classics and New Writing from Turkey*, from the Cunda International Workshop for Translators of Turkish Literature, 2006-2012 (Milet Publishing 2013). He and Saliha Paker also edited and co-translated much of *What Have You Carried Over? Poems of 42 Days and Other Works of Gülten Akın* (Talisman House Publishers 2013) as well as Turkish novelist Latife Tekin's *Dear Shameless Death* (Marion Boyars 2000) and *Swords of Ice* (Marion Boyars 2007).

ERIK MORTENSON is a Senior Lecturer at Wayne State University's Honors College. His translations have appeared in *Turkish Poetry Today, Asymptote,* and *Two Lines Press.* In addition to his work as a translator, he is the author of *Ambiguous Borderlands: Shadow Imagery in Cold War American Culture* (2016) and *Capturing the Beat Moment: Cultural Politics and the Poetics of Presence,* which won a CHOICE Outstanding Academic Title Award in 2011. He has recently finished a manuscript, tentatively titled *Translating Counterculture,* that examines the reception of the Beat Generation in Turkey.

EFE MURAD studied philosophy at Princeton and is currently working towards his Ph.D. in Ottoman History and Arabic Philosophy at Harvard. He has published five books of poetry, four books of poetry collaborations, and three books of translations from the Iranian poets M. Azad and Fereydoon Moshiri and from the American poets C. K. Williams, Susan Howe, and Lyn Hejinian in Turkish. Together with poet Sidney Wade, he prepared a selection of Melih Cevdet Anday's poetry in English, which won the Meral Divitçi Award for Turkish Poetry in Translation. His poems, writings and translations in English have appeared in journals including *The American Reader, Asymptote, Denver Quarterly, Five Points, Jacket, Poet Lore, Talisman,* and *Two Lines.* His poems appeared in an installation piece, *Pivot,* by the American-Pakistani artist Shahzia Sikander at the opening of the 13th Istanbul Biennial. He is currently working on the complete Turkish translations of Ezra Pound's *Cantos.*

MURAT NEMET-NEJAT is presently working on his poem *Camels & Weasels.* His recent publications include his translation from the Turkish poet Ece Ayhan *A Blind Cat Black* and *Orthodoxies* (Green Integer Press, 2015) and the essays *Holiness and Jewish Rebellion: 'Questions of Accent' Twenty Years Afterward* (University of Michigan Press, 2016) and *Dear Charles, Letters from a Turk: Mayan Letters, Herman Melville and Eda* (Spuyten Duyvil, 2016). Nemet-Nejat's poem *Animals of Dawn* will be published by Talisman House in the fall of 2016.

Gonca Özmen was born in Burdur, Turkey in 1982. She took her B.A. and M.A. degrees from the English Language and Literature Department of Istanbul University, where she is now studying for her PhD. Her first poem was published in 1997, and that year she was awarded the Yaşar Nabi Nayır Youth Prize and named 'a poet worth watching'. In 1999 she received the Ali Rıza Ertan Poetry Prize. In 2000 her first book of poetry *Kuytumda* (In My Nook) was published and won the Orhan Murat Arıburnu Poetry Prize. In 2003 Istanbul University honored her with the Berna Moran Poetry Prize, and in 2005 she won the Homeros Criticism Prize for an essay she wrote on the Turkish poet Edip Cansever. Her second book *Belki Sessiz* (Maybe Quiet) was published in February 2008. She has attended international conferences throughout Europe, and her poems have been translated into Spanish, French, English, German, Slovenian and Persian. *The Sea Within*, a selection of her poems translated by George Messo, was published by Shearsman Books in February 2011. She has been living in Istanbul since 2000.

Saliha Paker is a literary translator and Professor of Translation Studies who retired in 2008 from Boğaziçi University, where she still teaches a course in the PhD Programme. She founded the Cunda International Workshop for Translators of Turkish Literature in 2006 under the sponsorship of Boğaziçi University and the Turkish Ministry of Culture. Her translations include three novels by Latife Tekin, *Berji Kristin Tales from the Garbage Hills* (with Ruth Christie), *Dear Shameless Death* and *Swords of Ice* (with Mel Kenne), all published by Marion Boyars (1993, 2001, 2007), London/New York. She edited *Ash Divan, Selected Poems of Enis Batur*, brought out in 2006 by Talisman House Publishers, New Jersey, which also published *What Have You Carried Over? Selected Works of Gülten Akın*, co-edited with Mel Kenne, in 2014.

Arzu Eker Roditakis has a BA in Communication Studies from Istanbul University and an MA degree in Translation from Boğaziçi University, where she also started her doctoral studies, and gave courses on translation theory, practice and criticism. Her MA thesis, Publishing Translations in the Social Sciences since the 1980s: *An Alternative View of Culture Planning in Turkey*, was published by Lambert Academic Publishing in 2010. She currently resides in Greece, where she completed her PhD in translation studies at Aristotle University of Thessaloniki with a dissertation on the English translations of Orhan Pamuk's fiction. Since 2007, she has participated in the Cunda International Workshop for Translators of Turkish Literature, where she has collaborated in the translation of fiction and poetry into Greek and English. She is currently a freelance translator, instructor of English and Turkish, lecturer in translation studies, and independent researcher.

Zoë Skoulding is primarily a poet, though her work encompasses sound-based vocal performance, collaboration, translation, literary criticism, editing, and teaching creative writing. She lectures in the School of English at Bangor University, and has edited the international quarterly *Poetry Wales* since 2008. Her recent collections of poems are *The Museum of Disappearing Sounds* (Seren, 2013), *Remains of a Future City* (Seren, 2008) and *The Mirror Trade* (Seren, 2004). Her collaborative publications include *Dark Wires* with Ian Davidson (West House Books, 2007) and *From Here*, with Simonetta Moro (Dusie, 2008). She is a member of the collective Parking Non-Stop, whose CD *Species Corridor*, combining experimental soundscape with poetry and song, was released on the German label Klangbad in 2008.

Donny Smith's translations from Turkish poetry have appeared in the books *Pigeonwoman/Üvercinka* by Cemal Süreya (Indiana University Turkish Studies) and *I Too Went to the Hunt of a Deer* by Lâle Müldür (Artshop) and in the journals *Translation, Bitter Oleander, Metamorphoses, Artshop Çeviri, Ç. N.: Çeviri Edebiyatı*, and elsewhere. His translations from Spanish poetry have appeared in a variety of books and journals. He teaches at a high school in Istanbul.

Caroline Stockford is a translator of Turkish literature and poetry into English and Welsh. She also translates medieval Welsh poetry into Turkish and writes poems in English and Turkish.She has performed her work at the Eskişehir International Poetry Festival,
Stanza and twice at the Radnor Fringe Festival

Sidney Wade's sixth collection of poems, *Straits & Narrows*, was published by Persea Books in April 2013. Her seventh, *Bird Book*, is forthcoming from Atelier26 Books in late 2017. She has served as President of AWP and Secretary/Treasurer of ALTA and taught workshops in Poetry and Translation at the University of Florida's MFA@FLA program for 23 years.

Please go to our website to find more
poetry books and for
more *Turkish Poetry Today* issues

www.redhandbooks.co.uk